DO-IT-YOURSELFER'S GUIDE TO
VAN
CONVERSION

No. 992
$8.95

DO-IT-YOURSELFER'S GUIDE TO
VAN
CONVERSION

EDITORS OF "VAN WORLD"

TAB BOOKS
Blue Ridge Summit, Pa. 17214

FIRST EDITION

FIRST PRINTING— NOVEMBER 1977

Copyright © 1977 by TAB BOOKS

Printed in the United States
of America

Library of Congress Cataloging in Publication Data

Do-it-yourselfer's guide to van conversion.

Includes index.
1. Vans—Customizing. 2. Van world.
TL 255.D57   629.28'8'3   77-25195
ISBN 0-8306-7992-8
ISBN 0-8306-6992-2 pbk.

Preface

This book shows you how to transform a box-stock van into something you can be proud of, a rolling tribute to your skills, imagination, and abilities. Some readers may be interested in relatively simple mods, such as a hide-away bunk bed or adding an in-dash CB. Others will go all the way with a full-custom interior and multihued paint so deep you can fall into it. All this information and more is here, gathered from personal experience and from interviews with top-line commercial builders.

Chapter 1 takes a bare-bones Maxivan and shows you how to build an interior to your own specifications. Each aspect of the work is described from initial planning—in three dimensions—to cutting window holes and routing service lines. The next chapter takes you through CB installation and details antenna mounting techniques. Chapter 3 is all about stereo and speakers with professional tips on speaker location for best sound. Chapter 4 shows you how to install an aftermarket air conditioner—a must for down South vanners. By doing the work yourself you can save hundreds of dollars over factory air.

One of the big hassles is what to do about holes—holes left by unwanted body trim and windows as well as just plain rust holes. Chapter 5 gives you the skinny on how to cope with bodywork—with or without a welding torch. The next chapter is the whole story on fender flares, from late-model glass flares to homemade steel flares for early vans. Chapter 7 describes topside modifications and details roof rack and wing installation, with tips on proper wing trim for best traction and fuel mileage.

Chapter 8 was written over the shoulders of two of the finest van painters on the West Coast—Emmett Glasgow and Mike Love. Emmett takes you through the basics of a single-color enamel job from Bondo to the color coat. Mike shows you the sometimes arcane secrets of mural painting, toning, acetylene smoking, and flame design.

This material originally appeared in *Van World* magazine. In order of appearance, the authors are Rob Treichler, Suzanne Davidson, Chuck Koch, Gunnar Lindstrom, and Eric Pierce.

Contents

Chapter 1
Building Van Interiors

We built our van from scratch. No ready-made plans or prefabbed components in a box. We started with ideas of what it should be and do when it was done, and set out to design and build a van to fit those ideas.

We built it because we couldn't buy it. If you borrowed our floorplan, you'd have a copy of a van that was perfect...for someone else. And that's pointless, really. The idea, the justification, behind building your own van is to create for yourself the van that's perfect for you, a van that's unique and not just another variation on a theme that's been played 100,000 times before.

So we don't want to show you how to build...or rebuild Ski-Doodle. But follow along so that you can conceive, plan, design and build a uniquely different van that's just as right for you as Ski-Doodle is for us.

MAKE A SHOPPING LIST

First, what do you really want in a van? What does it really have to be, to be your van? Here are some of the features we put on our shopping list to make it uniquely ours. To fulfill our needs, Ski-Doodle had to:

—have sleeping and travel accommodations for five, since that's our family, and no one volunteered to stay at home.

—be comfortable at overnight temps of −20 to −30 degrees, for winter ski weekends, and have a freezeproof water system.

Fig. 1-1. The vanner's dream...a bare-bones van on which to express all your vanning ideas and originality. Not so bare-bones at that; new (in 1973) Dodge 300 Maxivan with heavy GVW package (8200 pounds), air conditioning power steering, power brakes, trailer towing package, two-tone high-gloss finish, deluxe chrome bumper and grille package. Yet to come: bubble top, living space for five, windows, vents, insulation.

—be self-contained, with refrigerator or icebox, stove and oven.

—provide adequate storage for five for extended vacation trips.

—have a toilet facility, since jogging to a cold one-holer at three ayem is not our idea of snow-country fun.

—be totally adequate in summertime as a boat trailer-hauler and free of overheating problems.

And finally, our van, whatever it was to be, had to have good to great road handling and drivability for weekend runs or long vacation trips. We'd had it with gigantic pickup campers that lumber and sway like drunken, pregnant elephants, and pulling a camp trailer was and is not our idea of icy road fun-time. Putting it all together without laying out the price of a second home, and fueling it without taking out a second mortgage on our first one, put the final details to our basic shopping list. Several salesmen told us, "If you want all that in one vehicle, you're just going to have to build it yourself."

WHERE DO YOU START?

You start with your own shopping list; write down all the things you want in your van, consolidating ideas from magazines, truck-ins, dealer displays and truck and auto shows. As the list grows, you'll weed what you need from the stuff you don't. The important consideration is getting your objectives down on paper. This can be an elaborate list, seemingly as impossible to fulfill as ours, or stated as simply as "...seats up front for three, with room in back for three bikes, tools, clothes and gear for a weekend of riding. An icebox for cold goodies, and water to wash up after a hard ride." Quick and easy as that sounds, this might be the basic design plan for someone's dream van. Five individuals could take the same list of objectives and create five entirely different vans. But that's what vanning's about!

Measure the van you've got, or the one you'll get. Measure the dimensions indicated in the accompanying diagrams, and note carefully the location of all interior posts, seat pedestals, gas-filler pipes, fenderwells, door openings and mechanisms (Figs. 1-2 and 1-3). If you can't move it, map it!

Turn this set of dimensions to a scale drawing using graph paper with quarter-inch squares. With each quarter-inch square representing three inches, your scale will be four squares or one inch per foot. Office supply stores can provide

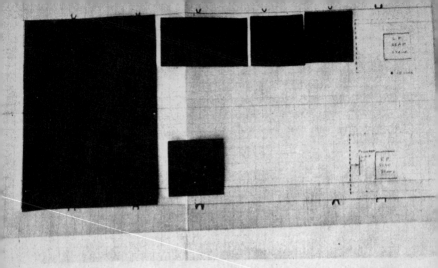

Fig. 1-2. With your internal dimensions reduced to your graph paper "blueprint" you're ready to do trial layouts using paper cutouts representing the items you feel you can't do without. Spaces in this trial layout represent the eventual layout of our Maxi Ski-Doodle and are, from left—bed/settee combination, (across top) double sink, four-burner stove, oven, Sani-Pottie enclosure/closet. At bottom, to right of bed, is refrigerator. A similar detailing was done for the overhead section of the extended top van.

Fig. 1-3. The next step refines the plan a bit further taking into consideration some components fitting under others, or building items over permanent obstructions such as wheel wells. Work also with side elevation diagrams to give yourself a better feeling for the final look of the project. Heavy dashed line at lower right is the travel limit of right passenger seat. Be careful of movable obstructions when taking initial measurements.

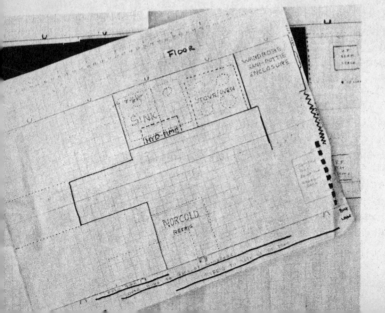

desk pad size (16 × 22 in.) graph paper at about 30 cents each. You'll need three to four sheets.

Next obtain rough exterior dimensions of all the items your van must have on your shopping list. You'll need length, width and height (or depth) of each item. (Note: Most gas-fired appliances require "space minimums" from walls, countertops, and other combustible materials. This required space, not only the physical dimensions of each item, must be considered in your design plan.) Want to tote two Hondas and a Kawasaki? Each one requires a T-shaped space, and you've got to determine the dimensions. Ditto sinks, Sani-Potties, iceboxes, tool chests, lounges, or extra seats.

BACK TO CHILDHOOD

With these dimensions down on paper, break out the ruler and colored paper, and cut blocks—yes, blocks—to represent the space requirements of the things you gotta have in the dream van. When they're all cut out, you play paper-doll house to determine the final layout of the van of your dreams. Design a set of the length and width dimensions (top view) in one color; a second set of height by width (side view—as seen from center aisle looking towards wall) in a contrasting color.

If you're planning to carry water, you'll need to plan room for a water tank and, if you wish, a waste-holding tank, but early in your planning, send away for catalogs and price sheets from Marine and Mobile Water Systems, 6400 Marina Drive, Long Beach, CA 90803. They make blank water tanks in virtually every size and shape imaginable. When you decide what space you'll be able to devote to the water tank, you tell them where you want the holes and fittings placed. Figure on $20 and up for a tank. Figure, too, on the weight of water—which is 62.5 pounds per cubic foot, and each cubic foot holds roughly 7.5 gallons (8.3 pounds per gallon). When a tank's half to three-quarters full, this is a lot of weight to go sloshing to the outside in a turn. If possible, locate water tanks low, and roughly amidships for best handling and ride.

AND NOW...YOUR FIRST MAJOR COMPROMISE!

In putting dreams on paper, it soon becomes apparent that all your good ideas simply won't fit in anything less than a Greyhound bus. The decisions made in this stage ultimately determine the overall look and personality of your finished van. Must that bar be three feet long, or will it look just as slick at two and a half? A seven-foot bed *would* be neat, but wouldn't one six feet six, plus room for a refrigerator, be even better?

In short, what can you, must you, do to make it truly a van you'll be able to say accurately reflects your tastes? For example, our main bed/dinette-table ensemble lies across the rear width of our Maxivan. No van builder could satisfy the mass population with a double bed this short, but we, both well under six feet, have no problems at all with a crosswise bed only 71 3/4 in. long. Making that one major compromise in the early design stage opened many layouts that would have been impossible had we insisted on a standard-sized bed placed lengthwise in the standard manner. When you design, you set your own standards. It's extremely important to note that when taking measurements, you measure only the actual space available; the difference in space between outer walls and paneled walls may well be five inches. Also, hip room (or lying-down room) will vary with the distance above the floor due to side-support curvature. Small amounts of space *do* count, especially when you try to put your six-foot-three bod in a six-foot-two bed. Never assume—measure!

DON'T CUT THAT HOLE—YET!

Before you lay a crowbar or chisel to the side of that $6000 bare-bones van in approximately the spot where you want a diamond or heart-shaped window, there are a few other preliminaries you should get out of the way. You've got a picture in your mind of how it's going to look when it's finished, and a rough layout of where things should fit. Now you'll need a working set of plans to tie things together.

Short of throwing six inches of foam and shag over everything, you'll need some sort of framework. To follow the contour of the wall exactly, paneling must be anchored to more than the side supports. Furnishings ideally should not rearrange themselves with every quick stop or lane change.

DESIGNING THE INTERIOR FRAME

Handiest framing material for the novice is 1 × 2, and though it looks spindly, if used properly, it is adequate to the task. If you've never worked with wood before, you should know that 1 × 2 actually measures 3/4 × 1 1/2 in., and you'll need to take wood thickness into account when drawing up your framing plans.

In creating a joint, remember the fasteners used (nails, screws, glue) primarily hold the joint together—the wood itself should carry and transmit the load. Know, too, that there are many better ways than these described here to join wood, but we're building a van with modest skills and tools.

WHAT TOOLS DO YOU REALLY NEED?

It would be nice to have a complete woodworking shop at your disposal, but you can build a van with much less. Ours was built with a minimum inventory of equipment, and the techniques we'll describe involve no expensive shop tools or exotic equipment. You'll need, besides basic hand tools (hammer, screwdrivers, pliers,etc.), an electric drill, assorted bits, electric saber saw, and assorted blades. You'll need a Stanley Surform half-round file,a carpenter's level and square, chalk line, and a handsaw capable of long, unwavering straight cuts. Not necessary, but about as nice as an extra pair of hands on a date with twins would be a mitre box that enables you to make precise angle cuts. In the final construction stages, you might be able to keep as many as six C-clamps working almost continually. Four-to six-inch sizes seem best for van work.

Now you're ready to design the framework. You can work with onionskin paper taped over your dimensioned diagrams, or directly on the graph paper, and figure, from the illustrations of sample joints, just how to put things together. When you've arrived at the final version, measuring the wood you need is an easy thing. Every inch on the paper is a linear foot of wood. Shop for price as well as quality, well before you start building.

TESTING YOUR PLAN

By now, that dream's starting to look a little less like a cloud and more like reality. Getting it down on paper does that.

But sometimes, the cake that's baked doesn't look like the one in the recipe book. Want a way to test your final design, for about a buck, and an hour's easy work, or less?

What you'll need is a roll of masking tape, a box cutter (single-edge razor in protective handle—hardware stores have them) and an armful of large cardboard boxes from the neighborhood supermarket.

Tape the actual interior dimensions of your van-to-be on any appropriate space, such as your living room floor. (But draw the drapes first—your neighbors will think you're nuts!) If you already have the van, use the empty interior. Cut down and tape the boxes to the overall size of your finished furnishings. The tape will hold the boxes where you want them. Now move around. (Have someone hold a broomstick at roof height if you're doing a living-room mockup.) Bend over to tie a shoelace. Is there a cabinet fighting your hip for space? Have breakfast in your van while thinking it over. Does your head inadvertently do a number on the stereo speaker when you try to start your day with O.J.? Can you eat your eggs without scrambling your elbow on the stereo or stove? A laid-back lifestyle is OK, but not if you have to lie back—literally—to see the scenery because the window doesn't line up with the world outside. If you must redesign, now's the least expensive time!

Though it's your van, others can contribute good ideas as well. Show your plans to other vanners. Not everyone will be ecstatic, but that's cool. You're not trying to sell them your camper, you're only looking for improvements. Listen for honest opinions and valid objections; if you come up with a strong reason for doing things your way, it's probably right, but if you wind up defending your ideas weakly, primarily because they're your ideas, you might possibly spend another hour at the drawing board. Designers sometimes get so close to their brainchildren they can't see the warts. They tell of an architect who designed a luxury condominium without elevators. The developer paid the architect's fee with a free 20-year lease—to the penthouse apartment! You'll have to live with your mistakes, too, so take your time.

You'll sometimes be torn between alternatives. Ask for other opinions. You might be surprised with what you get. I was torn between doors that swung up or down for the overhead cabinets. I asked for opinions and my 12-year-old said, "Why don't you make sliding doors? You can't hit your head on sliding doors, and sliding doors are fun." We have sliding doors.

Now you're finally ready to build! Well, not quite. Are you building in a sound system, water, LPG refrigerator, stove, or heater, or any electrical lines for additional lights and accessories? Now's the time, while the interior's bare. Plan wire, water, waste, and LPG line routings on transparencies taped over your interior layouts. Each inch on the drawings is a foot of required material; add approximately ten percent for items purchased in continuous lengths, such as wire; 15 to 20 percent more for things in sections as with ABS plastic pipe. Follow every line to build a complete parts list of all the supplies needed.

SOME LIGHT ON THE SUBJECT

Running more than one electrical circuit? Use a different color insulation for each, and detail the routing, and the color code, on your permanent interior plans so you'll know where to look if you need to find, or avoid, a wire in future alterations.

Each circuit should be suitably fused between accessories and battery, and it's not a bad idea to fuse the main service line from the battery to the fuse panel. Junkyards can supply main circuit fusible links and automotive dashboard fuse blocks that will split a main power lead from a battery into as many as six or seven separate fused lines. Buy good-quality wire fasteners, and crimp or solder the connectors carefully, and locate the fuse box where it's accessible if a fuse fails. You lose power with distance, so the route that takes the least wire is more efficient. If you're going to run more than one or two casual interior lights, you should consider an extra battery with an isolator switch wired into the charging circuit. This switch pulls power for accessories from the alternate battery without running down the main cranking battery, but lets the alternator charge both batteries when you're truckin'. Any trailer or supply house can help you with these switches. One manufacturer is Panoptic, 1795 Riverside Ave., Riverside, CA 92507.

SOME SOLID THINKING ABOUT HOLES

Water supply and waste lines can be roughed in, but you won't punch holes through to the exterior until your interior framing and paneling are completed. A hole misplaced even a quarter of an inch is hard to relocate.

Before the insulation or paneling goes in place, you should plan and lay out the exact location of windows and through-the-side connections. The fewer side-support posts you cut the better; so often a slight relocation of a window will result in fewer posts cut. When the location of any cut is pinpointed exactly, mark the corners by dimpling the metal with a sharp center punch. For circular openings, simply mark the center. *Do not* make cuts now, but lay out the cutlines on the inside of the metal panel and build a framework around the perimeter of the future hole. This frame will give the item solid support, something to attach to, and will prevent drumming and excessive flexing of wall and panel around windows and other openings. These frames should be as thick as the gap between outer wall and inner panel, and fastened with epoxy to the outer metal wall.

Where pillars will eventually be cut, make a V-shaped notch approximately two to three inches wide and two inches deep in the support pillar. The deepest part of the notch should be right over the proposed cutline.

For smaller openings, such as electrical connections, water service and drain lines, a block of scraps of sufficient depth which extends one and a half to two inches beyond all sides of the hole can be epoxied in place. When the hole is drilled, it will extend right through the block for proper support at that area.

MORE SOUND THINKING

Thinking stereo, quadraphonic, CB, TV, or any other trick electronics sometime in the future, but feel the lack of bucks now? Check out the sound store and ask the man what you'll eventually need to hook up your equipment, and put speaker wires and adequate power lines in place now. If you can afford speakers, it's often easier and more efficient to build them in than to add them later. Remember too, that any accessory or light mounted to anything other than part of the metal van body will need a ground wire attached firmly to metal, and routed to the mounting location. Attach these ground leads with self-tapping metal screws to interior ribs after scraping down to bare metal. Black is the commonly accepted color code for ground wires.

You'll avoid expensive hassles by getting out of the way all additions or modifications to the van underside or body that require welding or cutting. This includes trailer hitches welded to the frame, additional fuel tanks, and seam-filling or fender flares.

If future plans include trailer hauling, run necessary brake/flasher and running light wires now, before the paneling's in place. You'll find most recent American-made vehicles use the same line for brake lights and turn signals. You'll have trailer plug leads for:

1. right turn signal/right brake light and right tail lamps;
2. left turn signal/left brake light and left tail lamp;
3. clearance lights;
4. back-up light (optional).

GETTIN' IT ALL TOGETHER

Next step is converting the diagram into a detailed and itemized parts and materials list showing everything you'll need before the van is complete. If you know you'll need it, you might find it on sale at bargain prices. Start the habit of critical shopping (my wife calls it scrounging) and don't always look for items in the most obvious (and most expensive) place. Example: your neighborhood junkyard may turn up stoves, sinks, heaters from wrecked RVs at half new price.

Buy wood in the longest lengths you can handle and store for the least waste. Select wood carefully, and pass up pieces with excessive warp, twist, splits or moisture.

While you're shopping for ideas, collect parts catalogs from van or RV supply houses. Some will cost a couple of bucks; many dealers will refund against your first purchase. Most give dimensions for components, and these are helpful in the final planning and designing stages.

Grab good ideas wherever you can! Look over dealer display vans, and check inside cabinets and drawers for construction details. Chair or settee exceptionally comfortable? Make a quick rough sketch, complete with dimensions. Pay particular attention to such dimensions as: height from floor to seat, thickness of cushion, depths of seat, and angle and height of backrest. Is it a complete component you'd like to add? Check for manufacturer's name, address and model number.

Executive aircraft and luxury cabin cruisers are excellent idea sources for material selections and construction methods not typically found in RVs.

Super-ambitious? Check into adult education shop courses and the possibility of using evening class time with access to school shop tools for putting your dream on wheels. If you're a super salesman, you might even pull a Tom Sawyer and get the whole shop class turned on to your van as a class project.

FLOORING

OK! The big day arrives, and you're actually ready to start building.

To build a house, even on wheels, you need a foundation that's level.

Parking as flat as possible, make further leveling adjustments by jacking the lowest wheel(s) and shimming with the right combination of scrap boards and blocks till the van is level side to side and front to rear, indicated by the carpenter's level on the van floor. Note the exact position of each wheel and the thickness of the shims under each wheel, and you'll be able to level out again when you finish out the van's internal framing.

The floor should be good-quality hard particle board or plywood, at least 5/8 to 3/4 in. thick (Fig. 1-4). Before flooring,

Fig. 1-4. Ski-Doodle's floor was done with bits and pieces of 4-inch marine-ply jigsaw-puzzle pieced together; pieces came from a wrecked cruiser at cost of less than $3. If you're buying, make it from as few pieces as possible. Layout of 1 × 2 strips on floor is for right-side half of settee-bed combination. Spare epoxy from other fastening operations is being dabbed into screw countersink holes.

any wheelwell cracks or unnecessary holes in the metal floor should be patched by brazing, welding or with a fiberglass patch. For extra sound deadening and insulation, a commercial-grade jute or felt carpet pad can be installed under the wooden flooring. Leave a gap (3/16 to 1/4 in.) between the floor edge and the side supports. This gap should be the thickness needed to firmly grasp the panel you'll use. If you're applying material over panel, use the combined thickness of the panel plus two thicknesses of the material to be used.

The dead space behind the side supports should be floored with the same material epoxied or bolted in place. Take care that these pieces are even with, but do not extend beyond, a straight line between side supports. Line these up with a straightedge or chalkline. This gap will form a slot into which the paneling will fit at installation time. Leave sufficient clearance at rear so doors can be paneled, along with an additional 1/8-in. for edge trim molding. Check carefully to insure wooden flooring does not interfere with door-closing mechanism.

When bolting the floor down, you can avoid the needless embarrassment of drilling into fuel tanks, brake lines, and dead spaces by simply drilling upwards from the bottom side.

Make a special effort to avoid the knees of your topside helper, who will be countersinking each hole you drill and filling it with proper length machine screws of approximately 1/8 to 3/16 in. in diameter. Commercial van customizers generally anchor floors with self-tapping metal screws, but a good bolted hold-down will give longer squeak-free life, especially if you use flat washers between the nuts and metal floor. I used bolts about every foot. If you're buying a new van, wait till the conversion is completed before you undercoat it.

Tighten floor bolts in a sequence that starts out in midfloor, and work to both ends to avoid warping the floor. Keep the level handy during this operation to check on progress. A variable-speed drill with screwdriver bit will make quick work here. You'll need help underneath holding the nuts with wrench or pliers. Snug all bolts, then follow the same pattern to do final tightening.

PANELING AND INSULATION

You've seen the vans that gather every trophy imaginable for being ugly: gaps between sheets of panel show great gobs of insulating material settled to the floor line between panel and wall. It's not bad paneling, it's bad preparation. You can't hang a 4 × 8 panel with one screw in each corner and expect it to hang taut and wrinkle-free. While you're installing the floor and measuring and cutting furnishing framing, start preparing your walls for paneling. Epoxy straight-grained 1 × 2 scraps approximately three to four inches in length to each side of every interior post that will be paneled over. *Don't* make the edges flush with the post; instead, extend these scraps inward as much as 1/8 to 1/4 of an inch. Use a two-part epoxy such as Duro-Epoxe. Don't buy the little carded tubes, you'll be running to the store continually for refills. Instead, look for the larger cans; the product has an almost indefinite shelf life and you'll find it has dozens of uses. The wood/metal bond will be stronger if you first use rough grit sandpaper to break the smooth paint finish. Use C-clamps or a cross of masking tape to hold blocks securely in place while curing. Follow epoxy maker's recommendations; the stuff will not set properly in cold weather. It's a job for a moderate to warm day (65°F. or above).

When the blocks are set and cured (usually after 24 hours), file them to the contour of the post with a Stanley Surform half-round file. This will give an excellent surface on which to attach panel. You can also support crossbraces to similarly

Fig. 1-5. Left-half settee-bed combination shows simple frame construction technique and glued into position. This alternate method of plywood 1/2 in. sections as support members is a bit more costly, but simplifies framing tasks and gives nice divided storage areas. All construction at this stage is temporary, other than floor, and will be removed for final finishing, panel and insulation installation.

attached wooden blocks to act as brace points for interior furnishings, or additional paneling support. Build your furnishing framing, connecting only temporarily to the wall/framing system (Fig. 1-5). At this point in the construction, you'll merely cut and fit pieces, and hold temporarily without final gluing. Finishing nails with exposed heads can be used for easy removal later. Everything installed to this point, with the exception of flooring and epoxied wall supports, will again be removed before van completion. However, small, easy-to-handle cabinets can be fitted, disassembled, finished and reassembled permanently, except the final wall and floor attachments.

MEASURE TWICE, CUT ONCE

Your diagram should give you basic dimensions of the completed interior and a plan of how you'll put it together. Rather than trying to locate things relative to curved walls, make your locations relative to a precisely drawn centerline. Mark this line on the center of your drawing, and draw a corresponding centerline down your van centerline using a chalkline. (To use a chalkline, drive small finishing nails exactly on the centerline at opposite ends of the van floor. Pull the chalkline over the chalk, and tie line tautly to the two nails.

Pull the string upward about two inches, and let it snap. You'll have a faint blue line straight down the floor center.) Using a straightedge, retrace the line with an indelible marker. With a level floor, you can now ascertain true vertical with a carpenter's square or carpenter's level. Now cut and fit your framing per your preplanned diagrams, checking accuracy as you go with tape, level and square. The C-clamps also serve as extra hands to hold framing joints temporarily prior to final fitting and cutting.

With the framing for furnishings temporarily assembled, you can design and cut the patterns needed for the paneling or plywood to cover these frames. Make patterns for unusually shaped pieces on cardboard stock, and trim to perfection by trial-and-error scissor trimming. Very common first-time errors are pattern reversal or laying out a pattern with the grain running the wrong way. I made both. Best rule is to measure everything twice, and cut once.

Before disassembling the temporarily attached interior furnishings, mark all joints and pieces carefully so later reassembly, after sanding and finishing, will be easy. When they're marked, take everything out. It's time for insulation and paneling.

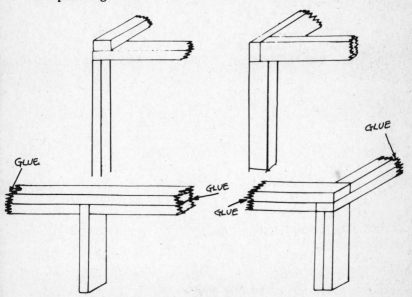

Fig. 1-6. There are several ways you can form joints with simple tools and 1×2 stock. Note how the load is borne by the upright member, not glue or fastening devices. When two pieces are used together, glue them together with white glue and clamp till dry for a strong bond.

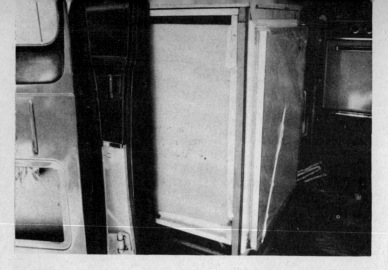

Fig. 1-7. Icebox installation with extra urethane foam insulation. All appliances were installed and connected, and the van was given some livability shakedown weekend trip-tests.

INSULATION

Insulation not only keeps you warmer in the winter, it will lessen the tendency of a van to act like an oven in summer, reduce body-panel noise by as much as 90 percent and make your van feel and sound much more solid. Depending on what you want your van to do for you, there are many kinds of insulation you can use. Since Ski-Doodle frequently hunkers down for the night at −20 to −30°F., we used one-inch urethane board, said to have as much insulating value as four inches of fiberglass (Fig. 1-7). Urethane, normally used in refrigerators, is about as rigid in board form as wall panel, and cuts beautifully by scoring and cracking. At approximately 28 cents per square foot (nine bucks for a 4 × 8 board), it's considerably more expensive than the average vanner wants or needs, but if cold-weather vanning is your thing, it's worth considering. Our rig, with two or three sleeping bodies, stays quite livable at 30° outside temperatures with only the pilot light of the Hydro-Flame furnace on. We'll maintain good warmth even at −20° with the 12,000 BTU furnace on less than halfway.

Probably better than urethane for sound deadening, though not as good for super-cold weather, is a board made of compressed styrene beads. Not to be confused with styrofoam, this bends quite easily, can be cut to shape by scoring and breaking and costs only about 13 cents per square foot in 1-in.

sheets. (Throughout the West, you'll find Tap Plastic Stores a good source of urethane and styrene plastic board. Tap has stores in San Jose, San Leandro, Concord, Sacramento, and San Mateo in California, and in Salt Lake City, Utah, and Portland, Oregon.)

The old standby, foil-backed fiberglass rolls, comes in 15 and 23 in. widths, and 3 1/2 and 6 in. thicknesses. Use the width that requires the least trimming for your support spacing. Standard lengths on fiberglass rolls are 56 feet for the 3 1/2 in. thickness, 32 for the 6 in., with cost factors of 11 cents per square foot for the 3 1/2 in.,20 cents per square foot for the 6-in. Cramming the 6 in. pack behind your paneling takes mucho muscle, but it's possible and pays dividends of a super-quiet ride. Commercial truck refrigeration firms (listed under "Truck Refrigeration Equipment" in the Yellow Pages) will also spray urethane foam in place in your bare van, but figure $200 to $300. A super way to go, but many bucks.

Attaching any of the board-type products is simple and easy with contact cement (Fig. 1-8). Follow manufacturer's instructions carefully, and work at the recommended temperatures. Best way to approach this project is to precut pieces to fit the whole van before beginning to cement. Use light chalk-marked numbers to key piece to location. If the day's a bit on the cool side, work on the sunny side of the van; on a warm day, you'll stretch setting time to a more comfortable limit if you work on the shady side, and can further cool the skin down by periodically rinsing the outside

Fig. 1-8. As insulation and other work progressed, blocks were continually epoxied to side pillars as attachment points for paneling. Note fuse box hanging on wall, and bundle of wires which service every light and appliance location throughout the van. Blocks above roof rail will hold track for overhead bunk.

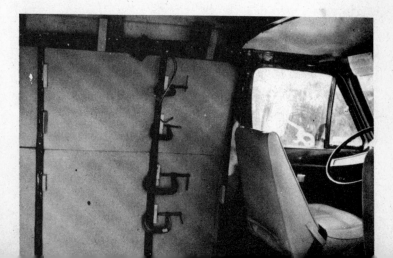

with a water hose. Contact cement is easily applied with brush or roller. Use inexpensive equipment and discard after use.

Working in the tight confines of a van, you can get an unhealthy high from the volatile fumes of contact cement. Work with all doors, vents and windows open and a fan pulling fumes out. Better yet, look around for some of the great new fume-free water-soluble contact cements such as Roberts 4120 Water Based Natural Contact Cement, at about $10 to $12 per gallon. Great stuff, and one gallon will hang all your insulation, hold carpet to the ceiling, and give you leftovers to touch up loose spots. Contact cements of all kinds are sold in industrial hardware stores, lumber and panel shops, and under "Carpet and Rug-Layers Equipment and Supplies" in the Yellow Pages.

FIBERGLASS TRICKS

There are two fairly easy ways of holding fiberglass pads in place on vertical walls. Both involve scissor-cutting the roll to as tight a fit as possible for openers. With one method, mash the pad toward the outer wall and tape the edges securely top and bottom and to side support poles with wide silver duct tape. Another method uses tack strips such as those used to hold down wall-to-wall carpet. Cut to fit the spaces between side pillars and epoxy in place right under the roof line and at ten-inch intervals down the van's side, with the nail points facing up. Hold in place with masking tape until the epoxy has cured, then hang fiberglass pads firmly in place on the rows of nails.

At this stage of the project, especially after you've done all the foundation work that needs to be done and have turned right around and stripped most of it back out, you're likely to be rather discouraged with everything.

Cheer up! You're probably better than 75-percent finished.

No windows, no cabinets, paneling, or furnishings...75-percent finished? It's true! And from now on, everything you do will go fast, and you'll see tremendous gains for every hour you spend working on that van.

If you've put furnishings—a settee, cabinet, or bar—against a wall, you'll actually panel the wall in two sections; above the attachment point, and below. If you're staying with low furnishings anchored only to the floor, paneling is easy and straightforward. In this case you might buy a set of paneling patterns to really speed the work.

Whether it's going to be paneled or upholstered in plush, or even fur and shag, anything you've done to ensure a good panel job will also insure a good plush finish. Plush walls, after all, are simply panels upon which you've installed some other material.

It's nice to have a little help with paneling because there are several four-handed jobs to the task. It's also nice to have someone to share your elation as you rapidly cover the bare walls. Or to blame if it doesn't go right.

Measure paneling vertical requirements by following the contour of the wall; if not, you'll wind up with a piece too short when you flex the panel inward. An easy way to measure is with a wheeled gadget used to install screening into aluminum frames (it looks like a pizza cutter). Clearly mark an index point on one part of the wheel, and start two inches up from the metal (not wooden) floor. (The wheel can't reach the floor.) Roll the cutter up the wall, carefully counting the revolutions. Count off the same number of revolutions on the panel, add the two-inch margin; that's it! The same tool can be used to score insulation boards for snapping.

Before slipping the panel into the bottom groove between the floor and the wall, mark with 3/4 in. masking tape on the sub-flooring and roof the exact location of the wood blocks on either side of the support pillars (Figs. 1-9 and 1-10). With the

Fig. 1-9. Paneling is cut to fit and checked for fit before disassembly and finishing of work outside van. Tape designates where paneling can be fastened to underside supports.

Fig. 1-10. Panel-fitting session before final nailing down takes place. Open area on wall will be paneled separately with another piece cut to fit under enclosure for sink/oven/stove and heater enclosure. No, that's not a cannon port, but the intake-exhaust fixture for the Hydro-Flame heater.

panel snapped in place, run a chalk line from the top to the bottom tape marks. This line will mark where you can drill to find good support for your panels. Pounding nails in may split the blocks or knock them loose. Drilling a small hole avoids both these problems. Start near the bottom of the panel and fasten all the way across, working upward as you go. Flexing panel in as you're driving screws is hard work and one of the places you'll appreciate an extra hand.

If you're using standard paneling, there is commercially available edge stripping, shaped much like the letter U and slightly longer on one side. This slips over the horizontal edges for a finished appearance. Use a thin bead of Elmer's Glue-All or other white glue to keep the molding secured to the panel.

Another useful product is plastic molding that butts two adjacent pieces together for a smooth, gap-free joint. It's shaped like the letter *I* and inserted between the butted ends of two adjoining panels. You'll find these plastic moldings in RV supply stores. There are other edge and seam treatments available, which we'll touch on later.

Paneling in plush is little different than paneling in wood, except that instead of merely fastening a panel in place, you'll be mounting a panel on which you've first attached carpeting, crushed velvet, fur, or whatever. Cut the panels to fit, remove and, flexing them slightly more than the amount they'll be when installed, attach the material firmly over the paneling. With less flex in the installed position, the material will be taut. Shag carpeting and deep plush can cover a multitude of sins and lack of craftsmanship (did you think there was another reason for its popularity?), and can be tacked or glued in place. The material is gathered around the back of the panel and stapled and/or glued in place. Certain shags and materials can also be contact-cemented directly on rough-finish paneling already in place. Before going ahead with this type construction on a van-wide basis, test a few sample swatches and glues. The test's not over till you've run it for several weeks, because some glues will run colors, become brittle and crack, or even deteriorate fabrics.

TIPS ABOUT PANEL CUTTING

Panel can be cut to fit with a saber saw, scored and snapped with a razor, or, if one is available, trimmed flawlessly in the most intricate patterns with a router. Good advice: before trying any method, practice on scrap stock. Experiment with several types of saber saw blades, and do layouts and cutting from the wrong (reverse) side, since you'll raise splinters on the side nearest the saw. Keep a good blade supply on hand; they're expendable. If you score and snap, use only the sharpest blades and cut deeply on the display side of the panel. This method requires a strong, steady hand, and lots of scrap stock practice. I personally found it darn-near impossible, though I've seen others get excellent results. If you're like most, you'll use a combination of several cutting techniques before you're through paneling.

Masking tape applied over the cut line on the display side of the panel reduces saw splintering and edge lifting.

Run a bead of Elmer's white glue in the floor groove for a good, secure fit.

There's quite a bit of waste and trimming in panel work, so buy enough to do the job and then some. Color and design may vary significantly from batch to batch, and a style may be discontinued without notice, making a good match impossible if you run out halfway through the job.

PANEL ALTERNATES

We like the look and feel of real wood and wanted to stay away from the production look of film-covered panel and Formica that is so *in* with the mass-market van converters.

We bought expensive luan mahogany-backed paneling for our cabinetry and used the smooth, knot-free panel backs for the display side. This gave us finished cabinet interiors (the outside was inside) and the backs took staining and finishing beautifully, using Deft Salem Maple Vinyl Wood Stain and several coats of Flecto Varathane Satin Finish with light sandings between coats. Our wall paneling was done in genuine wood—knotty pecan salvaged from an office at the best price—free! Similar panel today runs $16 to $20 per sheet. Besides giving the van the rich look and warm glow of wood, we have an easy-maintenance interior. Everything is washable; the surface reacts well to cleaners and damp cloth wipe-ups, and the dings and scrapes that invariably result when five people go trucking cross-country are easily retouched by a light steel-wool sanding, spot restaining, resanding and finally, a touchup of Varathane Satin Finish from an aerosol can. In many campers, every accumulated scratch, especially in vinyl film paneling, remains as long as you own the rig to continually remind you of the troubles it's seen.

KEEP THE WORK FLOWING

Take time in planning every step, and check plans and material lists before starting on each phase of work in your van. The greatest benefit of good planning is that it tends to keep the work flowing and makes the most of your time. It will also make the task more enjoyable. If you do it right, building will be almost as much fun as using your dream van.

You've got a van that's floored, insulated and paneled; a bunch of carefully marked, but unfinished parts lying in safe places around the pad; and little else for the hours you've invested in your van.

But you're better than 85-percent done! Believe it!

WOOD FINISHING

The effort required for furniture finishing—sanding, staining, resanding, and varnishing—can be cut by more than half by working on disassembled prefabricated units. Rather than sanding down into remote corners, you'll be able to twist and turn each individual piece exactly as you need it.

With a bit of planning, you can buzz through a great pile of finish work in very few hours.

Follow stain and finish makers' recommendations for the preparation of every stick of wood requiring finishing. Take the time to do it right; little scratches and flaws are magnified by staining and varnishing. If these skills are new to you, make a few practice runs on scrap to test the finished appearance of your efforts.

Do an assembly-line job on all the staining work. Stain can be applied by roller, brush, or a soft rag. Critical points in staining are a well-stirred product, properly prepared wood (some soft, open woods need priming; follow stainmaker's instructions), and the amount of time the stain is left on the stock. The longer it's left on before the excess is wiped off, the darker the stain becomes. Scrap experimentation may be the only way to get the results you want.

Most wood requires another light sanding after staining, since the water base in many stains raises the grain slightly. Varnish-type finish results suffer if you work them too much during application. Brush and stir lightly, and arrange a scrupulously clean, draft-free place for drying before you apply the finish, so the piece can be settled for drying with a minimum of handling.

You can get interesting effects by painting adjacent panels contrasting shades, or mixing painted panel with varnished or standard panel finish. We used a high-gloss *wet look* yellow enamel surface accented by stained-wood framing under the overhead cabinets. The glossy surface gives better lighting, and the color brightens up the dark area.

If all your internal furnishings will be of prefinished paneling, you'll need to finish very little wood, unless you want the satisfaction of knowing that even your cabinet interiors are finished. It's a nice, quality touch if you want to spend the time and effort.

Any framing that will show should be finished before reinstallation in the van. Support framing attached to the vehicle walls, if it will be visible after everything's bolted in place, should also be finished at this time.

After surface finishing, framing should be reinstalled, but at this stage of the game, joints, instead of being held with finishing nails or brads, should be drilled and countersunk, and fastened with flathead wood screws. You can countersink to the wood surface, and leave the heads flush, or countersink below the surface and cover with wood filler.

On final assembly, coat touching surfaces of every joint with a white glue such as Elmer's Glue-All. Clamp until dry. Protect the wood finish from the clamp jaws with scrap wood. Panel scraps are excellent for this purpose.

Fig. 1-11. Masking tape provides a good drawing surface for cut marks, protects paint during cutting operations.

CUTTING

With framing and wall paneling in place, but before cabinet paneling is installed, you're ready to cut up the metal skin of that beautiful van for accessory hookups such as water inlets and overflows, heater vents and windows.

First step is to tape the area of the cut completely for three to four inches outside the cut line and an inch or so inside as well (Fig. 1-11). Masking tape serves as a fine drawing board for precision cut lines, and also protects the paint surface from scratching by the saber saw.

Reference dimple marks are easily felt under the tape, and you'll be able to use these centers for plotting out exact cut marks. For large rectangular-shaped windows, you can use the chalkline to lay out precise straight lines, especially over slightly curved surfaces. Take your cutting dimensions from the actual item to be installed, and measure item and hole diagonals as well as sides (Fig. 1-12). This will help ensure that the hole is indeed as square as the window, and not slightly diamond-shaped. (Most decorative windows have instructions and templates. Follow the specific instructions exactly.)

With the cut lines marked out exactly, center-punch holes located 1/8 to 3/16-in. inside each corner, and drill at these

Fig. 1-12. Measure twice—cut once! Make all final measurements carefully, using measurements taken from the item to be installed, not from the manufacturer's instructions. Measure the diagonals also, to double-ensure that the hole is the same shape as the item to be installed.

locations with a fine drill approximately the diameter of a coat hanger (Fig. 1-13). Using an ice pick or sharp awl, poke a hole carefully through the insulation and panel. Use a square to ensure that the probe goes through perpendicular to the outer metal. If possible, have someone inside to protect the panel by applying pressure with a phone book. Enlarge these holes just enough so that they'll be easily seen. Drilling would be fine, but thin drills this long are rare.

With a larger drill bit (3/16 to 1/4 in.) redrill the holes from both metal and panel sides. At the minimum, they must be large enough to admit the saber saw blade. Ideally the hole should rest tangent to both cut lines.

Don't force the saw; hold it firmly against the metal to keep it from hopping, and guide it lightly forward. Try to feel developing binds before they cause the saw to jump. Keep firm control when going through pillars; you're cutting a maximum amount of metal for a small saw. Keep a good supply of fresh blades on hand; you'll probably break several.

File away any rough spots. Spray the bare exposed edge with any available metal enamel or primer to keep moisture from eventually working under the paint. If you've planned properly, the framing installed prior to insulation and paneling will be exactly around the window opening to keep the panel and outer wall from flexing at this opening. Shim up as necessary.

Place the window carefully in the opening. If it binds, and you have difficulty locating the bind, coat the window edge with carpenter's chalk and try again. The spot where you have a bind will be smudged with chalk. File it down and try once more.

FLAT WINDOW IN A CURVED VAN

Large windows are flat; fitting them to curved side panels seems to present insurmountable problems. Not to worry!

Fig. 1-13. Drill carefully, using deeply center-punched hole to prevent drill bit from skipping off across painted surfaces. Before removing the metal, drill or punch guide holes through interior paneling as described in the text.

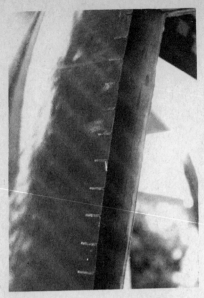

Fig. 1-14. Curved side walls will conform to flat window framing if you make cuts at one-inch intervals to within a quarter of an inch of the edge of the window flange. A bead of body "dum-dum" putty between the van surface and the window flange will give a weather-tight seal.

With the window touching the sides at the center, scribe screw holes on the masking tape. Center-punch the marks and drill with an appropriately sized bit for the self-tapping sheetmetal screw you'll use. It's best to drill test holes in scrap (the piece you just removed for the window is excellent) to insure a proper fit. When you've found the right bit, store it in the box of screws for future reference.

With the window again removed, mark off cut lines at 1 in. intervals, but avoid all screw holes by at least 3/8 in. (Fig. 1-14). These cut lines should extend from the window opening to within a 1/4 in. of the outside boundary of the window flange. These cuts will be needed on the vertical sides of the windows only, as the top and bottom of the window rest on relatively flat surfaces. Cut with a saber saw.

Tape the wood panel inside preparatory to cutting, carefully mark cut lines on the tape, enlarge the holes to blade size and cut with a blade style that minimizes splintering. Cut the panel in one piece; horizontal strips of the proper width can be used to make a sill that matches the wall. This sill can be attached with panel nails and white glue to the subframe between the panel and outer metal wall.

The same method of preparation, marking and cutting applies to all holes through the side skin. It's advisable not to leave masking tape on painted surfaces, especially in direct sunlight, any longer than necessary. Remove the tape as soon as cutting and protective painting is done. Should it dry and become brittle in place, rub with a soft cloth soaked in turpentine till it comes off. Before you install the window, clean the painted surface carefully and coat with good-quality automotive wax.

SEALING

You'll find rolls of body putty at RV shops. Unroll a strip around the window opening and set the window in place. Fasten the screws at the horizontal midline till snug, then tighten, in turn, screws above and below. In this way, the window will pull down to the metal side with minimum distortion. Tighten each screw only slightly each time and then tighten top and bottom rows of screws in a crisscross pattern from the middle to the sides.

The body putty will ooze out as you tighten, and will continue to ooze for several hours. The best tool for trimming is a dull butter or table knife. Incline the blade under the frame at about a 30° angle and trim. Save the excess; it comes in handy for plugging under-dash and firewall air leaks. If you never use the rear door, pack a bead of this stuff around the contact area and close the door on it. It will keep out dust, rain, wind, and noise.

The van's finally taking on a personality of its own, and though there have probably been changes along the way from the original concept, it's getting pretty close to your perfect van.

Everything done now is highly visible; hang a drape, put in carpet, lay down a cushion—the van takes on a finished appearance.

If you've waited till now to pick fabrics, take the van when you go shopping.

Most fabric shops will give sample swatches or snips of material, and from this you can get a vague idea what the finished interior will look like, but a swatch is nothing compared to the impact of a yard or more draped over a bare cushion, or held by a window. Once in the van with full-size samples, my wife and I both spotted almost instantly the combinations that accented and highlighted every wood and paint tone in the van.

UPHOLSTERY: A SEW-SEW JOB

Stitching seatcovers on a sewing machine is not difficult for someone familiar with the working end of Elias Howe's

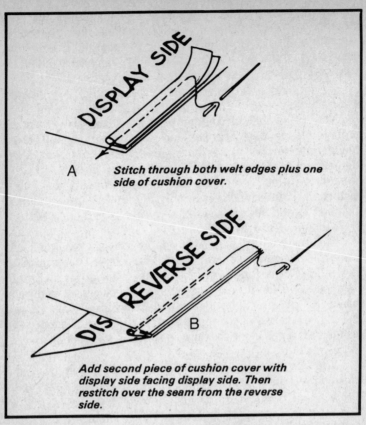

A. Stitch through both welt edges plus one side of cushion cover.

B. Add second piece of cushion cover with display side facing display side. Then restitch over the seam from the reverse side.

Fig. 1-15. Illustrations show how side and top pieces of cushions are to be joined. Machine sewing is not difficult, or you may have the job done at reasonable cost by an auto upholstery shop. Take the time and pains to do it right; this is one of the parts of the job that you'll always be looking at.

invention. Basically, covers are assembled inside-out and turned. Be sure to baste first—it will save many headaches later. The piping is joined to the right (display) side of the top piece by sewing a seam alongside the piping as close to it as the pressure foot will allow (Fig. 1-15A). The piping faces to the center of the material with the seam to the outer edges. The seam must be perfectly straight, then the side piece is laid on the top piece, right side facing right side. Pin together and restitch following the previous seam as a sewing guide (Fig. 1-15B). You'll repeat this with every seam.

Some of the smaller home machines will have difficulty with the heavy upholstery materials, but heavy-duty machines can be rented, or you can take cushions and materials to an auto upholstery shop and have them stitched up quite reasonably. If you have access to a machine, but no one to run it, go ahead; grab a handful of old rags and practice the techniques. Why not? If liberated chicks can change oil and do their own tuneups, you can run a sewing machine.

The clerks at yardage shops are generally very much into the practical side of the sewing business, and technically very knowledgeable about the proper techniques and materials. When you've made your selections of the materials you'll use, pump for information on putting it together. You'll get quality answers and technical advice.

FOAM YOUR HOME

Before you stitch and sew up cushion covers, you've got to have cushions to cover. Foam comes in all qualities, thicknesses, and densities; some gives more support in two inches than another will in three or four. Subject every foam to the sit test. Sit on the hard floor on a pad of the thickness you'll use; if you feel floor, you'll also feel bed or bench. We used a four-inch foam for dinette seat/bed cushions, and two-inch foam for all other bunks. Lying down distributes weight over a larger area than sitting and two inches of a good, dense foam is adequate for comfortable sleep. We found ours at TAP Plastic, mentioned earlier as a source for urethane and styrene board insulation. We'd shopped many sales offering bargain foam at low prices. What we found was no bargain; you can almost feel the date on a worn dime through three to four inches of much of it. Dense supportive foam is not inexpensive, but this is definitely not an area in which you should try to save pennies.

CUTTING FOAM

Cutting foam is one of the most frustrating experiences known if you lack a simple secret; once you know the secret, you won't want to stop!

Just about anything will cut foam—in a jagged line. Scissors, razors, and saws result in edges which look like they were trimmed by the star of *Jaws*. Compress the foam with anything and the line will waver relative to the amount of compression or twisting applied to the foam block while cutting.

Block out the shapes to be cut with a felt tip pen, barely touching the surface to draw the line. Too much pressure here will also produce a wavy line. Lay the foam block over the edge of a table with the cut line just outside the table edge. The

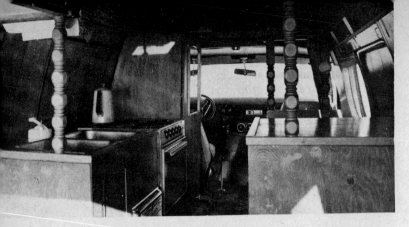

Fig. 1-16. Extensive use of natural woods distinguishes Ski-Doodle's interior. Layout is tight, compact. Turned columns are standard units purchased unfinished at building supply hardware store, and all serve a structural function. Poles behind passenger side seat give support to topside double-size bunk which pulls on rails at side of van. Lever at driver's right controls Hone Overdrive.

unsupported portion should be level with the table's edge without twisting, bending or squeezing during cutting.

Cut with an electric knife. Hold the blade perpendicular to the foam and let it cut at its own rate. If the blade is not forced, the cut will be perfectly straight and unwavering.

Don't throw away scraps! You can make large pieces from small ones by gluing the edges with spray contact cement, allowing it to dry till tacky, and pressing together. Ask for the cement where foam is sold.

DETAILING

You've almost completed the van. But if you've come this far, you'll realize you'll never be totally finished or totally satisfied with the results. There are always new ideas; some that can be adapted, some you'll file in the back of your head for the next dream van.

Getting close to completion is one of the real pleasures, because the little details, the accessories or the dress-up ideas you use will add the final sparkle that sets your van apart from the others.

In the final stretch, you'll have an almost finished unit that begs to be used, and use it you should, long before it's done. There are bugs and gremlins in even the most sanitary job, and there's no way better to find them out than by the acid test of truckin'. And no one better equipped than you to determine the actual problems and their solutions.

Take a simple thing like curtains. Need to screen off the front end, or cover windows for privacy and warmth in cold-weather camping?

You'll find a wealth of drapery hardware in yardage stores, department stores, decorating shops, bath shops, import stores, and dozens of other sources. You might even go to a hospital supply house for a special bendable track such as is used for privacy screening in hospital wards. RV shops also have van-scaled curtain track. But are drapes or curtains what you really want, or need?

Dark glass, such as is offered on the new Ford *nose* vans, can do away with the need for drapes. Or you can go the nylon film route. Small decorative windows are seldom curtained, but a trick way of attaching covers for nighttime privacy is with Velcro strips sewn to the hem of curtains and matching attachment pads fastened to van walls with epoxy.

Curtain rods can be attached directly to the panel with Molly-bolts.

The cap rail between the roof and the wall is a spot that gives many van builders fits. There are many treatments to finish this out in great style. Paneling can be cut to fit along the top and glued or nailed to blocks of scrap epoxied in at six- to eight-inch intervals.

Small mini-panels can be cut to fit and upholstered with cloth or Naugahyde-covered foam, for a thoughtful head-bump rail, especially over doors.

You can really dress up van interiors with ready-made moldings and lathe-turned spindles available at most builders' supply stores and lumberyards (Fig. 1-16). We used spindles for actual structural members for overhead cabinets, and they look a lot better than a plain two-by-four.

Fig. 1-17. Through these doors step the world's craziest skiers. Note carpet laid in place over tiled floor, edge molding on plywood flooring, storage locker under refrigerator for water-fill hose and electric power cords.

Fig. 1-18. Sink cabinet shows use of wood molding at top, plastic edging material on vertical corner. At left is plywood stained and finished, while front of cabinet (right) is reverse side of Luan mahogany paneling finished as described in text.

You can frame a window or a cabinet with a molding pattern miter box cut and glued to a plain door. Makes even plain-jane plywood look like a custom-made, hand-carved door.

Plywood is easy to work with for drawer fronts and cabinet doors, but an unfinished plywood edge doesn't really look super. Look for Flexible Wood Trim, by US Plywood, in lumberyards, panel shops and hardware stores (Fig. 1-17). This is a strip of wood veneer that's applied over a plywood edge with glue, trimmed, stained, and finished. It gives a professional appearance to plywood edges on cabinets.

Counter tops, bar tops, and table tops can be done in Formica laminate by cabinet shops at a reasonable price. We don't like the plastic look or feel of laminates, so we covered the counter around the sink and stove with casting resin (Fig. 1-18). We used 3/4-in. ply burned with a torch to raise the grain and stained under a 1/4 in. layer of resin.

Molding strips can also finish off counter edges, and provide ridges in cabinets to keep supplies from sliding about.

We used prefinished molding tracks for our overhead cabinet sliding doors, which were made from translucent plastic sheets. A nice feature of these doors is that they lift out for cabinet cleaning or stocking and give unlimited access through the length of the opening. We'll probably convert the lower seat cabinets to the same type of opening, using hard composition board instead of plastic. Vibration of one panel against another can be stopped by gluing felt pads to the panels in their overlap area.

We also fabricated an engine cover snack and drink tray using the Luan mahogany panel backs (Fig. 1-19). The top portion snaps onto the engine cover with a friction latch, and removes easily for cleaning spills underneath or for engine cover removal. Draw the pattern by tracing the engine cover outline on the wood.

FINALIZING THE FLOOR

Till now, the floor's bare, as it should be. There's no need to subject it to all the traffic and paint, epoxy, or glue droppings during van construction. Clean and sand it properly, and lift out any embedded foreign particles such as nails, sharp pebbles, etc. What you do with your floor next depends on how you want to cover it. One of our prime gripes with commercial RVs was the almost universal practice of permanently installed deep-pile shag, in many cases nailed to the floor before the installation of cabinets and furnishings. It looks nice, makes an easy installation and gives you carpeted

Fig. 1-19. Dash is essentially stock, except for owner-designed drink rack on doghouse, built with low profile to keep from blocking air conditioner flow. Top piece swivels up for map storage on trips, spill cleanup. (Pushbutton next to ignition key is propane choke for cold weather starts.) Vehicle runs on $.45-per-gallon propane. Toggle switch at upper left switches fuel gauge readout on dash from front to side tank.

cabinet floors, but, it makes the van look old years before its time when the carpet gets worn or even moderately tacky. The abuse Ski-Doodle can get in one weekend snow-skiing would rot three layers of shag before we got home. There's melted snow and ice, spilled food, and, during spring thaws, prodigious amounts of mud and even bits of parking lot tar to be ground in.

For these reasons, we opted for a vinyl tile floor covered in turn with wall-to-wall foam-backed indoor/outdoor carpet. Rather than attaching the carpet, it is merely cut to fit and laid in place, and therefore can be easily removed to shake out or for more thorough cleanings. The foam backing provides extra insulation and prevents creep. This carpeting is even amenable to outside cleanings with a garden hose, scrub brush and laundry detergent. In heavy use, we have found that this type of covering has lasted two to three years in previous RVs. Then we recarpet, using the old for a pattern. A standard 12-foot width will reach from the front seats to the tailgates of a Dodge Maxivan. Most vans can have floor covering for $30 or less.

Carpeting can be held down more permanently by the use of tack strips nailed to the subfloor, as in home installations, or double-backed carpet tape. Permanent carpeting should be installed over a foam or felt carpet pad for extra comfort, insulation, and wear.

Tiling, either with vinyl tiles or parquet (wood), is basically a simple task. The floor should be well sanded for either, and low spots filled—especially for vinyl, which will conform in time to any surface irregularity. Prepare the surface to the tile maker's recommendations, and use the adhesive recommended. Buy more than enough tile to do the job, and try to get all tiles for the job from the same batch, since color shades vary. Each box of tile has a batch number. Store away a few spares; they're handy when one gets cracked, broken, or stained.

Since we had planned on tile, the leftover epoxy from each construction task was dabbed in the countersink holes over bolt heads. As a final step, we sanded the floor smooth with a power sander, applied a leveling grout and tiled with adhesive-backed tiles.

Other possible floor treatments: for the man who wants a double-duty combination bike hauler and plush apartment on wheels, either snap or Velcro-fastened carpet over plain floor, or, a fitted canvas drop cloth with Velcro attachments over the permanently installed plush carpet. Canvas covers could be made to protect furnishings when the van's used for bike-hauling duties.

For the skier, surfer, skin diver: a false floor four to six inches off the metal floor. The air between floors would give an excellent insulation from cold intrusion, and the space, accessible through the rear doors, could be used as secure storage for surf or snow boards, boots, scuba gear, etc.

Split-level floors can be used to raise bed/lounging areas in the rear, with storage space accessible from inside the van for personal items, and through the rear doors for spare tires, jacks, chains, and tools. (There's no rule that says a spare has to be door-mounted.)

There is really no limit to what you can design your van to be. If the ultimate van is completed Tuesday, chances are it will be outdone by Wednesday.

When you build your own, you don't have to be satisfied with stock answers to standard needs. You build in the solutions you want at the price you can afford. You can build with the materials and textures you want at the pace and price that's most comfortable. You can avail yourself of ready-made components, or design and create your own.

The truly individualized van because it answers needs particular to one owner, is a unique collection of features that simply wouldn't be available commercially. Here's a short list of items in Ski-Doodle, and some of the design criteria behind each one. They might provide ideas for your dream van.

Internal Water-Fill: I'd spent several particularly unful-filling weekends removing well-buried water tanks from previous RVs to clean out dirt, pebbles, mudpies, and other garbage deumped there by adolescents possessed of a malevolent nature and too musch spare time. Solution: Make the water-fill accessible only through the inside of the vehicle. Eliminates one more outside obstruction, too!

Portable Chemical Toilet: Designing sleeping space for five in a van didn't allow for a permanent toilet with plumbed-in holding tank. While traveling, we generally use public facilities. The toilet is set in the aisle between the two front seats when the van is camped. The open closet door and the curtains affords a reasonable amount of privacy. We've also found the Sani-Pottie to be trouble- and odor-free, unlike the more complicated and expensive recirculating chemical toilets. We like the ease of dumping the Sani-Pottie too. No hoses to hook up, no looking for dump stations. The unit can

Fig. 1-20. Owner-builder applies one of the last pieces of shag carpet tile to plastic bubbletop. Carpet is decorative, sound-deadening and a good insulant against heat and cold, prevents condensation in cold campouts. Wires to ceiling fluorescent fixtures were run in notch gouged from carpet backing foam. Carpet was applied with contact cement to tiles and top.

easily be dumped in any toilet and refilled at any water hose. (Sani-Pottie — Mansfield Sanitary, Inc., 150 First St., Perrysville, OH 44864.)

Freezeproof Water System: We routed all our water lines along inner walls rather than follow traditional RV builders' approach of routing water lines along the outside wall. In addition, the water tank, pump, and lines are all within three feet of the exhaust/inlet pipe of the Hydro-Flame 12,000-BTU heater. The system has sucessfully weathered freezeups at even − 30 degrees.

Operating Economy/Handling: The one-ton van was purchased with heavy-duty suspension and trailer towing/air-conditioning packages. We replaced the original tires with Michelin eight-ply 8.00 × 16.5 rubber, going for maximum mileage rather than looks. We even traded down to skinny six-inch-wide rims at Michelin's suggestion for better handling and tire life. It may not look like you like, but the tires, at 45,000, look like they'll go to 60,000. We're still filling up at $0.45 per gallon, or less. Ski-Doodle burns propane, and that means an engine that will last at least 200,000 miles with no major problems. Mileage is 9.8, not bad for a high-top 6800 lb. bus. Propane carburetion is by Impco, 16916 Gridley Place, Cerritos, CA 90701; tanks (39.5 gallons rear, 25.2 side) by Manchester, 2880 Norton Ave., Lynwood, CA 90262. We get good acceleration and hill-climbing ability, plus boat-pulling traction with the Dodge 4:10 rear axle. For economy and less

44

engine revs, we cruise effortlessly with a Hone Overdrive spliced into the driveline. (Hone Overdrive, 11748 E. Washington Blvd., Santa Fe Springs, CA 90670.)

Carpeted Ceiling: Any conductive surface simultaneously exposed to freezing temperatures on one side and warmth on the other will have a condensation problem. Halfway through our van project, and before we carpeted the roof, we had icicles form during an overnight campout at − 10 degrees. We contact-cemented shag carpet tiles (manufacturer's seconds—17 cents each—defective glue backs) with foam backing to the ceiling (Fig. 1-20). They're decorative, have excellent insulating quality (both shag and foam act as dead air space), and are easy to clean with a vacuum cleaner. We've also kept windows to a minimum for the same reason. Window-icing can be controlled by a combination of moderate heat and good air circulation, with restricted airflow to glassed-in areas. We use heavy curtains to seal off the front end of the camper; this area may be 25 to 30 degrees cooler than the living space after a cold night.

The Hydro-Flame furnace has a blower attachment which we use primarily during high winds to keep the van warm and draft-free. (Hydro-Flame, 1874 Pioneer Rd., Salt Lake City, UT 84104.)

Fig. 1-21. Ski-Doodle in its current finished form. No trick wheels or tires, and a basically uncluttered exterior, but a van that's everything its owner wanted. Unit is used extensively for skiing, and is comfortable in sub-zero campouts, due in part to few windows and super-efficient 12,000-BTU heater. Self-contained, Ski-Doodle has a go-anywhere, camp-anywhere ability, and lack of large windows allows hassle-free campouts along the route on long trips.

Refrigeration Insulation: Our icebox enclosure wraps an extra inch of urethane foam about the icebox's own excellent insulation. As a result, a 25-lb. ice cake generally lasts the better part of three days, even in 90 to 100-degree temps. We make ice in milk containers in the home freezer, and this serves well for our weekend trips. The only time ice must be purchased is on trips of longer duration in the summer. In winter camping, we pop in a shovel or two of Mother Nature's own snow. It's plentiful and the price is right. The double insulation is a well worthwhile tip that could benefit other vanners, especially those trucking through the desert.

There are, unquestionably, many sources and materials we've not touched on, but that is part of the personality of vanning. The only way to really personalize that van is with your ideas, your methods and your materials (Fig. 1-21).

Now the rest is up to you. We'll be anxious to see your results.

Chapter 2
CB Installation—
Drop It In, Turn On, Tune In

For those of you ever-eager post-pubescent vanners who can't wait to "do it yourself," here is something to do in the privacy of your own van, that is quick, easy and most gratifying afterwards. What is it? Why, installing your own AM/FM eight-track stereo with CB radio, of course. What a relief it will be when you finish and know that it was done right. Right?

This particular unit is the Audiovox TCBH (Fig. 2-1) and is an in-dash unit. While not exactly theft-proof, the in-dash sets usually discourage thieves since, if they snatch the unit, they have to take the dash along with them. Not only that, but the TCBH microphone easily disconnects. Once it's removed, the unit gives the appearance of a mere radio. But enough of the aftereffects. On to the joy of installation.

First things first. Wash your hands. Now, remove the engine cover and the dash plate. The van we were working on was a Chevy, but steps are similar for all vans. Slide the radio up sideways behind the dash (Fig. 2-2). Then turn the radio around and pull it through the existing holes in the dashboard, with the nuts going on the base of each control knob stem (Fig. 2-3). In case you get lost, the model comes complete with an instruction manual.

The next step is the speaker installation. You have to make sure that your choice of an area on the van does not interfere with the window operation (Fig. 2-4). Once the section is circled it can be cut out (Fig. 2-5).

Fig. 2-1. Here is the Audiovox TCBH 23-channel CB, with AM/FM eight-track stereo.

Drill a hole in the door for the speaker wires, with a corresponding hole in the door jamb (Figs. 2-6 and 2-7). Now string the wires up to the radio (Fig. 2-9). All of these wires are color-coded, which makes it easier to install.

Once you have finished the above, the antenna can be installed. For the A-pillar-mounted antenna, you must drill a hole in the body A-pillar (Fig. 2-10). The antenna wire is put through the drilled hole and the antenna is screwed down (Fig. 2-11). Then the antenna and power wires are hooked up to the radio with the ground wire attached to a bare metal screw (Fig. 2-12). Now, you're almost finished; just hook the speaker wire to the speaker, and mount the speaker on the door (Fig. 2-13). That's it!

Fig. 2-2. Here the engine cover and dash plate are removed and the radio is slid up sideways.

Fig. 2-3. The radio is turned around and pulled through the existing holes in the dashboard with the nuts going on the base of each control knob stem.

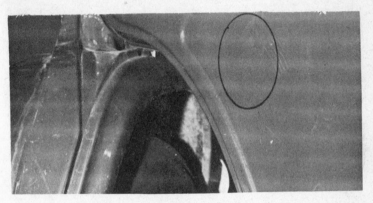

Fig. 2-4. Circle shows new home for speaker. Make sure there will be no interference with window operation.

Fig. 2-5. Cut out the circle. You'll need something stronger than pinking shears.

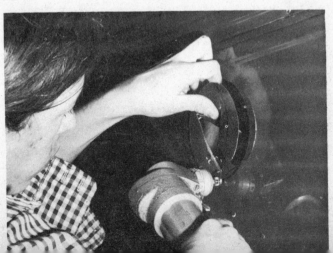

Fig. 2-6. Drilling a hole in the door for the speaker wire.

Fig. 2-7. Corresponding hole in door jamb for hole in door.

Fig. 2-8. Stringing wire through two door holes.

Fig. 2-9. Hooking up speaker wires to the radio.

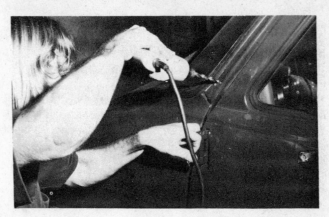

Fig. 2-10. Put antenna on by first drilling hole in the body A-pillar.

Fig. 2-11. After putting antenna wire through hole drilled, the antenna is screwed down.

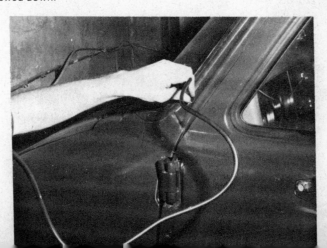

Fig. 2-12. Hooking up the antenna and power wires to the radio. You go straight to the fuse box and draw power, hook the ground wire to a bare metal screw.

Simple, uh? Now don't you feel all tingly? OK, go wash your hands. We used side-mounted antenna for convenience and ease of installation. But if you want to make the best of that CB's half-watt, the only way to go is topside (Fig. 2-14).

Ideally you should mount the antenna as high as possible with few, if any, obstructions around it. On a van the best antenna location is smack in the middle of the roof, since this provides a good ground plane and decent signal reach in all directions. Mounting an antenna at the corners of a vehicle tends to make the transmitted signal more directional in nature. Remember this: if the antenna is located toward the front of the van, the signal is elongated to transmit farther to the rear, and vice versa.

When mounting the antenna, make sure you have a good ground. Too many mobile installations have poor grounds and therefore insufficient ground planes which result in impaired

Fig. 2-13. After hooking speaker wire to the speaker, mount the speaker on the door.

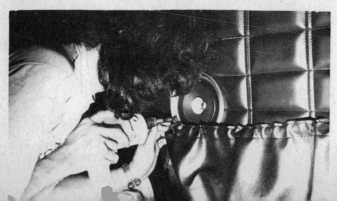

Fig. 2-14. Roof-mounted antenna with halo (optional).

Fig. 2-15. The General Motors base-loaded antenna, number 994466, comes with all hardware and has both roof and trunk mounts.

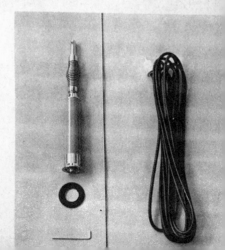

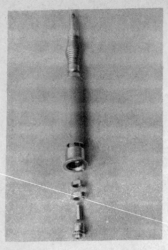

Fig. 2-16. Before installation, the base of the antenna must be disassembled.

Fig. 2-17. Begin the roof mount installation by drilling a 3/8 in. hole in the center of the van's roof and running the coaxial cable through it.

performance. Bare metal-to-metal contact is best for a good ground and one way to ensure this is to scrape off the body paint where the antenna base meets the roof.

For this rig, we decided a roof-mounted base-loaded antenna was best and installed a General Motors unit part number 994466, on a Chevy van (Fig. 2-15). It is a simple

Fig. 2-18. Strip off the outside insulation cover of the cable for 1 1/4 in., leave approximately a quarter of an inch of the steel braid intact and trim the remainder down to the copper core.

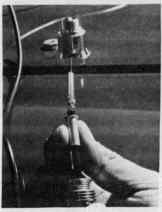

Fig. 2-19. Insert the stripped end of the cable through the bottom section of the disassembled base and then slide the sleeve over the cable until it is flush with the bottom.

Fig. 2-20. Push the slotted end of the base assembly containing the antenna cable through the roof hole and tighten the double threaded nut until the base is securely mounted.

Fig. 2-21. Spread the steel braid so it covers the top nut of the base assembly. Then insert the exposed end of the copper wire through the capping nut and tighten so the braid is firmly clamped in place.

procedure requiring a minimum of tools, only one hole, and 20 minutes. If you follow the procedures detailed in Figs. 2-16 through 2-23, you'll be assured of getting your ears on straight.

Fig. 2-22. Place the rubber pad over the bottom section so it rests on the roof and screw the chrome base onto the bottom section of the mount.

Fig. 2-23. Screw the loaded coil onto the chrome base and insert the antenna whip. The antenna can be tuned by moving the whip up or down and tightening the set screw with an Allen wrench.

Chapter 3

Surround Yourself
With Sound!

Few of us are content with an AM radio. Usually an AM/FM stereo radio is considered "bare minimum" by way of equipment, with AM/FM/eight track or cassette a more likely combination.

And, with the advent of compact automotive four-channel sound systems, another advance in electronic technology has appeared: AM/FM/eight-track Quad! Likewise, the quality of sound these units are capable of reproducing has improved right along with the number of modes and features. Only time will tell how much audio wizardry can be packed into a box small enough to fit the little hole in the dashboard of a van.

It's ironic, that while most vanners are able to elaborate on the specifications, features, and performance of sophisticated in-dash units they are relatively unschooled in the other—and equally important—part of the total system: the speakers. This lack of knowledge has caused vanners to have second-class sound even though they've installed a first-class audio unit. Many, for instance, simply upgrade the player unit and wire it into the same old speakers. Others, while willing to spend bucks for a multi-function high-output player, "economize" by purchasing bargain speakers. And a few pay more attention to mounting their speakers where they *look* good and not enough to locating them where they *sound* good, too. In most cases, the unit itself takes the blame.

If you're less than satisfied with the sounds in your van, a second look at your speakers is in order. To coin a phrase, "a chain is only as strong as its weakest link." From bitter experience we know that speakers are that "weakest link" in van sound systems. While it may seem like an impossible task at first, the proper choice and installation of speakers for *you* and *your van* isn't as difficult as you might think.

CONSULT A PROFESSIONAL

The first step is to consult a stereo dealer familiar with vans. If possible, consult two or more dealers, taking your van with you each time. A good dealer will be equipped to allow you to listen to several sets of speakers and be able to tell you of the pros and cons of each speaker and speaker type (Fig. 3-1). If you've chosen a good dealer, he's probably set up many vans similar to yours in the past and will have a pretty good idea of what you'll like—and what you won't.

LISTEN—AND LEARN

Once you've found a dealer—or two dealers—that meet your requirements, take the time to listen, both to them and to the speakers they have on display. Your own ears are the best judge of the kind of sound you want. Sound quality varies dramatically between brands and models even within the same price category. Some speakers are more responsive in the high, or treble, end of the tonal spectrum while others are more responsive in the lower, or bass, areas. The frequency range specs (your dealer should have these available on each

Fig. 3-1. One of but several demonstration boards at North Hollywood Stereo, this gadget allows the customer to switch from speaker to speaker quickly to compare sound characteristics.

Fig. 3-2. Regular (left) and coaxial (right) speaker types in the 6×9-inch size. Both types are also available in smaller 5 1/4-inch round size.

speaker he sells—if not, write to the manufacturer) are often helpful here.

For instance, if you like more treble (high-frequency response), a speaker with a frequency range of 100—12,000 Hz might be a good choice. For those who like more bass (low-frequency response), a speaker with a frequency range of 50—10,000 Hz would be most pleasing. Even within these ranges there are different responses. Again, let your ears be your guide.

Magnet size, often thought of as a measure of speaker quality, is more accurately a measure of the depth, or "fullness," of sound. Generally speaking, the larger the magnet the fuller the sound produced by that speaker—within limits, of course. Most experts agree that magnet weight of more than 20 ounces is wasteful, and one that weighs less than ten ounces is probably inadequate for the job. If you like a full sound, your speakers should have magnets in the 15- to 20-ounce range in the 5 1/4 in. round and 6 × 9 in. oval types.

High-output speakers come in two flavors: regular and coaxial (Fig. 3-2). Regular speakers are usually single-cone designs with the high-frequency sounds produced by a dome in the center. The dome may have a smaller cone surrounding it for more amplification.

Coaxial speakers, on the other hand, are two separate speakers within the same frame, one on top of the other. The larger of the two produces the bass while the smaller cone, suspended within the larger one, produces the treble. Not only does the coaxial design give better separation between the highs and the lows, the overall frequency range is often greater than with a single-cone design.

OTHER CONSIDERATIONS

Once you've decided which speakers you like best, there are other considerations that are just as important. First, check the speaker impedance against the output load of your player. If the output load of the unit is within the impedance range of the speaker (usually two to eight ohms), the two are compatible. If not, pass on those speakers. Second, check the power capacity of the speaker, in watts, against the *per channel* audio output of your player. If the output of your unit (usually about eight watts per channel) is less than the power capacity of the speaker, the player and the speakers are compatible. If not, pass on the speakers. Third, check that there is enough space in your van to mount the speakers you have chosen.

SPEAKER LOCATION

Just as important as making the proper choice of speakers is the proper placement of the speakers within your van. The location of the speakers can make or break the quality of sound they produce.

While customized vans have individual problems, there are some guidelines for speaker location that apply to any interior. Both of the experts we asked (T&H Van Works and North Hollywood Stereo) agreed about speaker location. Two 5 1/4 in. speakers in the doors and two 6 × 9 in. speakers in the upper rear corners are optimum (Fig. 3-3). But dividers, curtains, furniture, etc., act as baffles. Take the baffle effect into consideration but be careful not to lose sight of the basic layout concept.

Installing the rear speakers shouldn't pose any problems, but the ones in the forward doors must be positioned carefully so that there is no interference with the window mechanism. On Dodge vans, the speaker should be approximately halfway down on the door panel and eight to ten inches aft the forward edge. On Fords and Chevys the speaker goes two-thirds of the way down. *Measure your own van for your own speakers* to be absolutely certain that everything will clear before cutting the holes.

WIRING

Wiring speakers is easy so long as a couple of things are kept in mind. First, read the directions that come with the

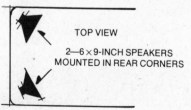

TOP VIEW

2—6 × 9-INCH SPEAKERS
MOUNTED IN REAR CORNERS

Fig. 3-3. T&H Van Works recommends this layout for best sound quality.

speakers and player unit. Second, use only top-quality speaker wire and connectors, making sure that each connection is as strong as you can make it. Use solder whenever possible. Third, connect the positive input lead to the positive speaker terminal, and the negative lead to the negative terminal. Reversing the leads will interfere with sound quality and volume. Fourth, wire four-speaker systems in series, and with the rear speakers grounded to the chassis or body of the van. Four-speaker systems should use compatible eight-ohm speakers in both front and rear for best results.

BE PREPARED TO SPEND SOME BUCKS

If you want good sound, you've got to be willing to pay for it—both for the speaker *and* for the player unit. Plan to spend from $25 to $55 per pair for speakers. According to the folks at T&H Van Works and North Hollywood Stereo, the following speakers have proved themselves:

5 1/4 in. Round

Arkay ten-ounce round
Audiovox SC10 and SC20
Craig 9420 and 9427
Jensen 20-ounce coaxial or regular
Pioneer 160 and 161

6 × 9 in. Oval

Craig 9542 (coaxial) and
9422 (regular)
Jensen 20-ounce coaxial or regular
Pioneer TS693

Chapter 4
Cool It!

Ah yes, summer. That time of year when the sun shines brighter, and hotter, and the interior of your van assumes the personality of an oven with temperatures to match. Sitting in the driver's chair while the heat slowly fuses your skin to the vinyl upholstery and watching steam rise from the cold beer in your hand, you wonder how you can cool the interior.

Already you've punched holes and installed sunroofs, vents and, super scoops. But these measures serve only to circulate the outside air inside and do not substantially lower temperature levels. Compounding the problem is the fact that factory air conditioning costs nigh on $600 and, if you're like most of us, you took a pass on this option when your van was purchased. So, you sit there and perspire, hoping it won't get too hot or that the genuine African pith helmet you just bought helps stave off heat stroke.

Don't despair for too long. There is a solution if you are willing to part with a few dollars—and one hot summer will probably make you quite willing. After-market air conditioning which looks much like original factory equipment is available. The A.R.A. Manufacturing Co., 602 Fountain Parkway, Grand Prairie, Texas, makes a custom *in-dash* air conditioner for most vans that has an installed price some $200 less (depending on locale) than its factory counterpart (Fig. 4-1). To see how it's done, we took a 1976 Chevy van to Van Nuys Auto Air, 7631 Van Nuys Blvd., Van Nuys, CA, and watched while a unit was installed.

Fig. 4-1. Before installation of the A.R.A. air conditioner, the Chevy van's dashboard had the empty recesses used for factory air. The A.R.A. unit is designed to utilize them also.

Since the A.R.A. air conditioner comes complete with all hoses, fittings, ducts, etc., and has a detailed set of instructions (Fig. 4-2), it is possible to do the installation yourself (thereby saving a bit more) if you are handy with tools and have a spare weekend.

To begin the installation, disconnect the battery, remove the engine cover, and discard the right side heater flex hose. Using the paper templates supplied with the kit, trace the outline of the three dashboard air ducts and cut them out, being careful to file the edges after removal (Figs. 4-3 and 4-4). Drill a 1-in.-diameter hole in the dash below the heater control panel, insert the wiring harness and capillary tube of the switch panel assembly in the hole and then screw the panel in place under the heater controls (Figs. 4-5 and 4-6). Then two 1 1/2 in. diameter holes must be drilled in the firewall to the right of the engine cowling.

The dashboard is loosened and removed (Fig. 4-7). Trim the right end off the right bottom dash brace where it is bent and place the supplied mounting bracket into the channel of the brace in a downward position. Trim a 2 1/2 in. long by 1 in.

Fig. 4-2. The A.R.A. system comes complete with all the equipment and hardware needed for installation. Cost is much less than factory air.

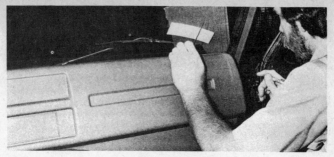

Fig. 4-3. Paper templates are suppled to trace the outlines of holes to be cut in the dashboard for louver assemblies.

deep piece from the right bottom of the dash and replace the modified right side dash brace with the original hardware (Fig. 4-8).

Insert the left side air duct's hose adapter through the hole cut in the dashboard and place the louver plate over it. Secure the entire assembly with four screws (Fig. 4-9). The passenger's side louver assembly is now put in its respective hole as is the center hose adapter.

Drill two 1 1/2 in. diameter holes in the right side flooring (Fig. 4-10). After connecting the refrigerant hoses to the evaporator case and covering the exposed metal with tape, place the case in the cavity between the dashboard and firewall and route the two refrigerant hoses through the holes previously drilled in the firewall (Fig. 4-11). Attach the top portion of the evaporator case to the dash panel using the original dash clips and two sheetmetal screws.

Fig. 4-4. After the hole's location is traced, cut and trim being careful to file the edges smooth.

Fig. 4-5. Drill a 1-inch diameter hole in the dashboard under the heater control panel.

Fig. 4-6. Insert the wiring harness from the air conditioner's switch panel into the 1 in. hole and then fasten the panel in place with screws.

Fig. 4-7. The next step is to loosen the dashboard and partially remove it from its location.

Fig. 4-9. Following the installation of the air duct adapters in the dash holes, place the evaporator case in the dash cavity and secure with screws. Run the flex hose from the evaporator to the air duct adapters.

Fig. 4-8. Trim a 2 1/2 × 1 in. piece from the bottom right corner of the dash through which the heater hose will be routed.

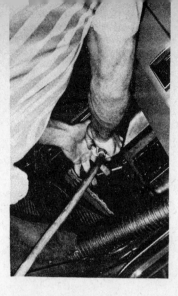

Fig. 4-10. Drill two 1 1/2 in. diameter holes in the right side flooring next to the engine cover.

Four wireform flex hoses come with the A.R.A. unit. Three of these are routed from the evaporator case to the center and left side air duct adapters (no hose is needed for the passenger side outlet). The fourth hose runs over the blower housing to the right side kick panel and connects to the heater outlet.

To reinstall the dashboard, shove the flexible defroster ducts towards the firewall while pushing the dash panel back as far as possible and replace all the bolts and screws on the left side. Next, push back on the lower right side of the dashboard, drill two holes in the kick panel to attach the dash panel brace, and drill two more holes in the bottom of the dash

Fig. 4-11. Route the two refrigerant hoses from the evaporator case through the previously drilled holes.

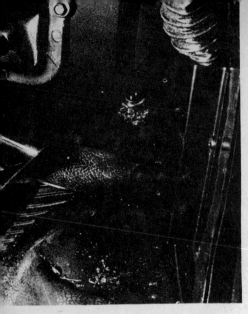

Fig. 4-12. To accommodate the condensate drain hoses, drill 9/16 in. diameter holes in the passenger's flooring and insert the hose.

to match those in the evaporator's mounting bracket and secure the unit with sheetmetal screws.

The dash panel installation phase is completed by placing the heater hose bracket on the right kick panel in line with the existing holes and securing with screws. Then replace the original heater hose cover using the stock hardware and attach the louver assembly to the center air duct. Next, drill 9/16 in. diameter holes in the floorboard and route the condensate drain hoses from the evaporator through them (Fig. 4-12). Running the blower motor's black power lead wire to the fuse box, attaching the brown ground wire to any convenient metal surface, replacing the engine cowling, and

Fig. 4-13. In the engine compartment, the fan and shroud must be removed before work is begun. Then bolt on the compressor belt pulley adapter.

Fig. 4-14. The compressor mounting brackets are attached to the engine using already existing bolt holes in the cylinder block and head.

Fig. 4-15. The compressor body is then fastened to the mounts and aligned with the belt pulley.

reconnecting the battery complete the interior installation portion of the project.

In the engine compartment you must mount the compressor, condenser, and the receiver-drier. With the fan, shroud and all belts removed, attach the compressor belt pully adapter to the bottom pulley of the engine (Fig. 4-13). Then

Fig. 4-16. With the grille removed, the condenser is mounted in front of the radiator, maintaining at least a half-inch clearance between the two.

Fig. 4-17. The receiver-drier is now installed to the left of the condenser. The refrigerant hoses are routed through holes in the grille backing plate and connected, then the grille is replaced.

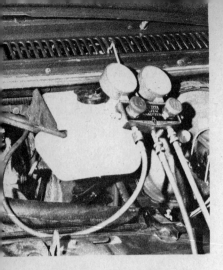

Fig. 4-18. The final phase of the installation is to charge the system with Freon.

Fig. 4-19. As installed, the A.R.A. in-dash air conditioner has the look of original factory equipment.

bolt the compressor-mounting brackets into existing holes in the cylinder block and left cylinder head and fasten down the compressor (Figs. 4-14 and 4-15).

To install the condenser, first remove the grille. Place the condenser in front of the radiator making sure the two are at least a half-inch apart. Once located properly, bolt the condenser in place using the attached brackets (Fig. 4-15). To the left of the condenser mount the receiver-drier. Connect the larger of the refrigerant hoses from the evaporator to the compressor suction valve. The smaller hose runs from the evaporator to the receiver-drier and on to the condenser (Fig. 4-17). The remaining hose is routed to the compressor discharge valve from the condenser.

The installation is completed by attaching the blue clutch wire to the compressor; fitting the fan, alternator, and compressor belts; reinstalling the fan and shroud; replacing the grille; and charging the system with the Freon (Fig. 4-18).

To see the pros do it, the A.R.A. installation takes about three hours. However, plan on a full day if you do it yourself. Either way, the result is a neatly packaged in-dash air conditioner which is almost impossible to distinguish from the factory unit (Fig. 4-19). And, when you turn on the three-speed fan and feel the rush of refrigerated air, you'll know that your van's interior cooling problem is solved—at a considerably lower cost than you might have thought possible.

Chapter 5
Basic Bodywork

The clean look is definitely "in." Side trim and factory names have got to go, and the holes under them must be filled. The traditional nose and deck job is brazed—a technique that works well for small holes, particularily if the holes are located on a curved panel (Figs. 5-1 and 5-4). Just about any klutz can braze a trim hole closed when turned loose with a torch and a length of brazing rod. Brazing the hole closed without warping the panel, however, is entirely another matter. This is especially true of van panels, as they tend to be broad, flat, and prone to showing every ripple—especially when painted dark colors.

Because Bondo is expensive and ripples are ugly, the idea is to braze the hole closed without warping the panel any more than is absolutely necessary. At this point I'm sure somebody will pop up and say, "But a really good professional body man can do it without warping the panel at *all*." Well...maybe. But then, if you could afford to have a pro cherry out your beat-up van you probably wouldn't be reading this book in the first place, right?

COOLING

Anyway, the idea is to keep the panel on which you are working as cool as possible while at the same time allowing the area immediately surrounding the hole to get hot enough to let the brass bond well to the parent metal. This will isolate any warpage within the area around the hole and will help prevent

Fig. 5-1. While earlier Dodges had clean hoods, the latest ones have big, ugly, chrome letters.

the entire panel from being ruined. The localized warpage may be nearly eliminated too, but we'll get to that later.

The low-bucks way of keeping the panel cool is the application of rags or towels soaked with cold water to the panel surrounding the work area. To do this successfully you've got to have either ten hands or a couple of willing friends to help hold the water-soaked rags against the panel while you weld up the hole (Fig. 5-5). Surround the hole with wet rags at a distance of four to six inches, covering as much of the surface of the panel as possible. Keep a bucket of cold water at your feet, too, with a couple of good-sized rags in it—you'll need them. Adjust the torch to a brazing flame using a small tip (number 00 usually works well), being very careful not to use too much oxygen as this makes the braze very brittle and usually results in a pitted and sloppy weld, too.

BRAZING

When filling the hole with rod, work as quickly as possible because the wet rags can only absorb so much heat before they allow it to spread to the rest of the panel. Likewise, attempt to

70

Fig. 5-2. To remove letters, simply back off the self-tapping nuts and lift off.

fill only one hole at a time on any given panel to prevent an accumulation of heat in the work area. Very small trim holes may be filled by heating the entire circumference cherry-red, applying the rod to the center of the hole, and allowing the brass to spread of its own accord (Fig. 5-6). Larger holes, those designed for the side-trim clips, must be treated slightly differently. Heat the entire hole but concentrate the heat on just one side, the side that will receive the rod first. By laying the rod *across* the hole, favoring the heated side, rather than applying it from a near vertical angle, more of the rod will be deposited quicker—thus lessening the chance of overheating the area. It's always a good idea to practice on a spare fender or door to perfect your technique rather than taking the chance of warping your van due to inexperience. Minor pinholes in the

Fig. 5-3. Grind paint from work area to help adhesion; be careful not to overheat metal and cause it to warp.

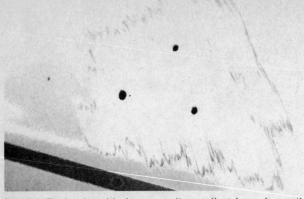

Fig. 5-4. Dodge hood holes are quite small and may be easily filled with braze. Large holes must be plugged with steel plug.

braze needn't be of great concern; once cleaned of brazing flux, they may safely be filled with Bondo during the final smoothing stages.

Holes larger than those used for sidetrim clips should not be closed with braze alone. A snugly fitting plug, made from similar gauge sheetmetal, should be fashioned to fill the hole flush with the surrounding metal and brazed into place. This method is preferable if the area is to be redrilled or worked in any manner. An alternate method is to cut the plug slightly larger than the hole to be filled, hold it in place from the backside, and then braze it in from the front. This alternate method is a little cruder and requires a little more Bondo to

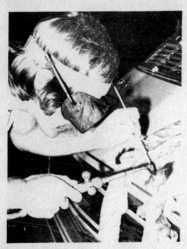

Fig. 5-5. Once brazing technique is mastered the job will go quickly. More than one person is usually required.

72

Fig. 5-6. Finished braze should look something like this. Proper oxygen/acetylene mixture and tip are important.

finish, but is also faster and requires less skill in welding and metal work. In either case, tack the plug in place first, allowing plenty of time between tacks to let the area cool down. Wet rags should always be used around the work area to prevent the welding heat from spreading to the rest of the panel.

SHRINKING

Once the hole is filled, quickly move the torch away from the work area, pick up a large water-soaked rag from the bucket at your feet and apply it directly to the work area while it's still hot (Fig. 5-7). The application of the cold rag to the cherry-red work area will shrink the heat-expanded metal back into its original contour—or nearly so. If done correctly, this will result in a repair with minor distortion within an area less than six inches across.

Before attempting to dolly the small amount of distortion out of the repair area, allow it to cool thoroughly and then

Fig. 5-7. Once hole is filled, quench work area quickly to shrink metal back to the original contour.

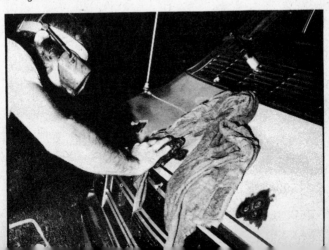

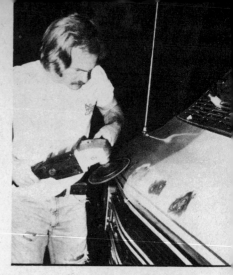

Fig. 5-8. Be careful when grinding braze smooth that area is not overheated.

grind the brazed hole smooth with a body grinder (Fig. 5-8). Be very careful not to heat the metal excessively while grinding, as this will tend to further warp the area. The grinding will also serve to point out the high and low spots in the work area (Fig. 5-9).

If you were a little slow on the draw with the cold rag after brazing, you'll find the area very difficult to dolly smooth. It's likely that the area will "oilcan" (pop in and out) when you push on it. These conditions indicate an incomplete shrink. To eliminate this problem you must carefully reheat the area—keeping the heated area very small—and apply the cold rags again until it smooths easily and no longer "oilcans." A final bit of work with the hammer and dolly should smooth things out so that only a very thin skim of Bondo is needed to surface the area. Remember: minor low areas may be filled with Bondo but high spots may not. They must be dollied flush with or below the surface level.

Fig. 5-9. Hole filled and ready for Bondo "skim coat," final sanding and preparation for finish paint.

BONDO

Back in the middle '50s when Bondo (a name brand at that time) made its first appearance, it had its problems, as most infant products do. It would often separate after being on the car for some time, lose its grip on the parent metal, and fall off with a thud. It was also common for Bondo to absorb moisture, causing the parent metal to rust underneath. Again, the thud of Bondo hitting the ground.

Even today it's not uncommon to see cars and vans with areas where the Bondo has separated from the metal body, causing an ugly hole or dent in what would otherwise be a fairly cherry body panel. And, since it's much easier to blame the failure on the Bondo than on the owner's lack of preparation, the product gets a bad name.

As with any automotive repair, there are tricks to the proper use of Bondo on an auto body. These tricks are very often the difference between a permanent repair and a "quicky" repair that will eventually fail with a resounding, and familiar, "thud." It is, of course, impossible to cover all the little tricks to the successful use of Bondo in a book of this type. We will, however, make an attempt to cover the important aspects one at a time as space permits and will give enough information so that nearly any budding body man can make his own repairs as a professional would.

BUBBLES

A great many otherwise successful body repairs have been spoiled by lack of attention to just one detail: cleanliness. While this statement is generally true, it is never more true than when applying Bondo to a panel that has been previously brazed—as in the case of filling the holes that remain after the removal of side trim and ornaments. Most readers have, at one time or another, seen the effects of the reaction between Bondo and an unclean brazed panel—known as "Bondo blisters" or "bubbles." These bubbles, which appear anywhere from a couple of weeks to several months after the repair has been made, completely ruin the appearance of the panel—and the car, too.

"Bondo bubbles" are caused by a chemical reaction between the brazing flux and the Bondo itself. This chemical reaction causes the Bondo to decompose chemically, losing both its grip on the parent metal and its hardness, so that, in advanced stages, Bondo bubbles may be the consistency of cornstarch under the thin layer of exterior paint.

Proper preparation of the brazed panel will prevent Bondo bubbles by eliminating their cause. By removing any brazing flux residue on the panel, the cause of the bubbles will have been removed as well. Sounds simple, doesn't it? Unfortunately, however, that's not the case.

CLEANING THE PANELS

First, the braze must be ground down to the level of the surrounding metal with a disc grinder and coarse disc. Be careful in this operation that the metal is not heated to the point that it will warp the panel that you were so careful not to warp during the brazing process.

Unless you are unusually skilled in brazing, there are bound to be pits in the braze and discolored areas on the metal next to the brazed area. It is these pits and discolored areas that hide the flux that many nonprofessional repairmen miss, thus allowing the bubbles to form.

Using an awl or other pointed tool, dig down into *all* the pits to rid them of flux. The flux is glass-like in texture and varies in color from black through brown and amber to clear, and is often invisible to the eye. By digging each pit out very carefully with the awl until only bright brass is left, the repairman may be fairly sure that little flux remains. Likewise, all discolored areas should be carefully scraped so that absolutely nothing but bright metal, either brass or steel, remains. Then, just to be double-sure, take a stiff wire brush and scrub the area well until it shines, letting the bristles dig down into the pits. At this point you can be sure that the area is clean enough that the Bondo will adhere well and that no bubbles will form later to spoil an otherwise slick repair.

APPLYING

From this point the Bondo may be mixed and applied in the normal manner, being very certain that the catalyst has been thoroughly mixed into the filler. Improperly mixed or inadequately blended Bondo will leave soft spots in the repair that will make sanding difficult and may cause eventual failure. Likewise, if one coat of Bondo is not sufficient to fill the depression, be sure to sand the first coat thoroughly before adding the second and any additional coats. Bondo will not adhere well to the slick surface of unsanded previous coats—nor will it adhere well to any dust remaining after the surface has been sanded.

Bondo work is not at all difficult and may be successfully done by any backyard body man. The material itself has, in the past several years, been improved to the point that if all work is done carefully with a critical eye towards cleanliness, there is no reason to doubt that a Bondo repair will last as long as the car to which it has been applied.

COLD FILLING

While brazing works very well on the Dodge hood—as it would on any well-supported curved surface—it is not really the hot tip for at-home repairs on large surfaces by a body-work novice. The problem is, of course, that the heat from the torch tends to warp large flat areas (and large curved ones, too) even though the utmost care is used to prevent this occurrence. Even some professionals have to resort to an overabundance of Bondo to cure the warpage caused by a moment's carelessness or inattention.

Because the holes left in this early Chevyvan's roof—following the removal of the ladder racks installed by the telephone company when the van was new—were in an easily warped area, we decided to fill them without the use of a torch (Fig. 5-10). The method we chose puts quality hole-filling within reach of readers not skilled in the use of a torch and who have only a minimum of tools at their disposal. This procedure will work equally well for round holes of nearly any size, and in nearly any portion of the van's body so long as they are accessible from the back.

The first thing that comes to mind is to grind the area of the hole clean of paint and slap on some Bondo, right? Wrong! Modern Bondo is great stuff, but just filling the holes without any support from behind is asking more than even modern

Fig. 5-10. First, grind off the paint with a body-grinder around the hole—or in this case holes—down to the bare metal.

Fig. 5-11. Use bolts that fit snugly into the hole, then reduce their head size by grinding, and use locking fluid.

"miracle mud" is capable of doing. While it may look great for a while, sooner or later it'll loosen from vibration, crack around the edges, and possibly even fall out.

BOLT-IN-THE-HOLE TRICK

The trick, then, is to find a quick and easy way to support the Bondo spread over the hole—to reduce the stress placed on the material and, at the same time, provide a larger bonding surface. While other methods were tried, we decided to do the old bolt-in-the-hole trick for a quick, easy, and durable job.

The first step is to grind the area of the hole to be filled and as large an area around it as possible—at least six inches for best results. Then, after selecting a short bolt that fits snugly in the hole, grind the bolt head so that it is approximately 1/8 in. thick—thin enough to be covered easily but still thick enough to be held securely by a wrench (Figs. 5-11 and 5-12).

Fig. 5-12. Install the bolts and tighten them down securely.

Then, using Loctite Bearing Mount or a similar material on the threads to prevent the nut from loosening later, tighten the bolt in the hole.

Once all the bolts are securely in place, find a short length of heavy wall 1 1/2 in. tubing or pipe and a hammer. While the next operation is not difficult, a certain amount of care must be exercised so as not to do more damage than good—a word to the wise. Holding the length of pipe over the nut on the back side, use the hammer to recess the bolt head—and a small area of the surrounding sheetmetal—below the level of the panel's surface (Fig. 5-13). A straightedge is helpful to determine the point at which this has been accomplished. Be careful not to recess the bolt head further than you have to, as this will tend to distort the surrounding sheet metal more than is necessary. If you've done everything correctly, only a 1 1/2 in. circle (the same size as the pipe you've used behind the panel) will be recessed, but that's plenty to give the Bondo a good surface with which to bond.

Once all the bolts have been recessed a batch of Bondo may be mixed and applied to the whole area (Fig. 5-14). With the help of a "Bondo board" and 80-grit sandpaper the whole works can easily be smoothed so that, once primed and painted, no trace of the former holes remains.

WINDOW HOLES

Bolts work OK for the small stuff, but the biggies require something else. Holes for ventilators, holes for service hatches, and, the most common, holes for extra windows must be filled with steel.

Fig. 5-13. Recess the bolt head with a hammer, using a heavy piece of 1 1/2-in. tubing on the back side.

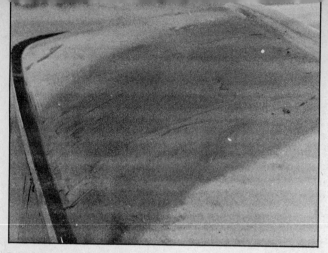

Fig. 5-14. When done, get the Bondo out and over the whole area, being sure no bubbles remain around bolt heads.

Our particular Chevy, an ex-telephone company van, for instance, had a window installed in the passenger side rear quarter panel that matched—but not exactly—the original equipment windows in the side doors (Fig. 5-15). It was installed, presumably, for additional vision to the right side but, due to the braces in the area, didn't really work all that well.

Since the extra window was both useless as well as ugly, we decided that it had to go. This is all well and good in theory, but in practice there are a few problems, one of which being how to fill the hole left when we removed the window. Sure, we could cut a piece of sheetmetal the same size as the hole and weld it into place. But, since a van's sides are large, unsupported areas of sheetmetal, they tend to warp at the sight of a torch. So, resigned to the fact that it should preferably be filled without heat, we started looking around for materials that would best suit our needs and the needs of readers who have similar holes in similar places.

PRELIMINARIES

After a great deal of footwork, we found an epoxy-type adhesive that could be made to work, called 3M Scotch Weld Structural Adhesive (#2216). Because this adhesive is an epoxy, it needs both time and heat to cure, but once cured it's as strong as a weld and can't warp off the panels. During the curing process, two conditions must be met for the adhesive to perform properly. First, the pieces to be bonded must be held tightly together by means of a clamp, screws, or rivets. And

80

second, the temperature must not drop below 60 degrees during the 24-hour curing period. Other than that, it's just the same as any other adhesive.

The first step after removing the window (which, fortunately, had been carefully installed without distorting the surrounding metal) was to gather the necessary tools and supplies together so that we wouldn't have to stop working until it was finished (Fig. 5-16). We borrowed a good body grinder from a friend so any paint, rust, and crud could be quickly and easily removed. While a smaller sander would've worked OK, the body grinder made a quick job of it. The 3M Scotch Weld was obtained through the local 3M distributor (a two-ounce tube kit was enough for the one window).

To hold things together while the adhesive was curing, we obtained a box of small screws with shallow countersunk heads, a sharp drill bit of the proper size, and a countersink bit with the correct angle for the screws. Finally, a trip to a local surplus store and seven bucks produced a 24 by 48 in. sheet of 18-gauge sheetmetal—cut to the exact shape of our window opening with a "nibbler" by the store manager according to a template we had brought along—and enough excess to make the backing panel (Fig. 5-17).

Fig. 5-15. The offending window, though it matched in size and shape, is far from attractive or appropriate for a custom van.

Fig. 5-16. Removing the glass was easy, just take out the locking strip that fits in the groove and push 'er out.

TO WORK

With the window removed, the borrowed body grinder was put into service removing paint, rust, burrs, and crud from around the edges of the window opening and extending about

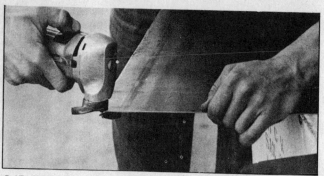

Fig. 5-17. A nibbler is almost a necessity when the patch is shaped, as it does not distort the metal being cut.

Fig. 5-18. The surrounding area was first checked for warpage (there was none), then ground for good Bondo adhesion.

four inches outward (Figs. 5-18 and 5-19). The grinder was also used to smooth up both sides of the patch itself and one side of the backing panel, the one that'll receive the adhesive (Fig.

Fig. 5-19. The inside was carefully ground, also, so that the adhesive would get a good grip on the metal and not loosen later.

Fig. 5-20. Both the patch and the backing panel were ground on both sides for good adhesion of epoxy and Bondo.

5-20). Working slowly and carefully to minimize the gap, the patch was hand-filed so that it fit perfectly within the opening on the side of the van. The backing panel, too, was trimmed so that it fit well on the backside and cleared all braces and other obstructions.

Then, holding the backing panel in place, the shape of the opening was traced from the outside so that the patch could be properly placed on the backing panel and epoxied into position. We had decided that it would be best to first epoxy the patch to the backing panel and then install the two onto the van as a unit. To bond the patch to the backing panel, we first drilled four holes, one at each corner of the patch, through both the patch and the backing panel, so that proper positioning could be maintained and to help hold the two tightly together during the bonding process. We then spread a thin coating of adhesive on both pieces, set them together and put the screws and nuts in place (Figs. 5-21 and 5-22). Once the four screws were tightened down, the unit was placed near a furnace with a heavy toolbox on top and left to cure overnight.

The following day, the unit was carried to the waiting van and placed into position so that the fit could be checked and the holes for the positioning screws could be drilled. If everything checks out OK, put the four positioning screws, one in each corner of the backing panel next to the window opening, in place and tighten them down. It's very likely that there will be some gaps between the backing panel and the inside surface of the body. It's a good idea to install several additional screws along each edge to insure that the patch and the body will be held together firmly so that the adhesive will achieve a good bond. Once you're satisfied that they're held firmly enough,

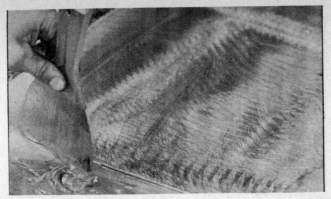

Fig. 5-21. The Scotch Weld was mixed and applied—according to directions—on both surfaces to be bonded together.

take all the screws out and apply the adhesive to the bonding surfaces, put the patch unit back into place, reinstall the screws and tighten them down.

To help the patch match the contour of the van's side more closely, brace it from the back side with whatever's handy (Fig. 5-23). This will insure a better adhesive bond and also minimize the amount of Bondo necessary to smooth the whole thing off on the outside. Also, you'd better have either a warm garage or an electric heater located inside the van to be sure that the patch temperature doesn't drop below 60 while the adhesive cures overnight.

FINISHING UP

Once the patch has been bonded to the van and sufficiently cured, the braces may be removed and the finish work begun

Fig. 5-22. The stuff is very easy to work with but must be applied thinly and evenly over the mating surfaces.

Fig. 5-23. Once the patch/backing panel unit has been bolted in place, a few braces will help the shape conform more closely to van's.

on the outside. Although the screws used to hold the patch in position may be removed, we chose to leave them in position as a little extra vibration insurance. Since the heads were countersunk when they were installed, we merely touched them up with a grinder and Bondoed over the whole shootin'

Fig. 5-24. Once the epoxy has set up thoroughly, the outside receives a thin coat of Bondo to fill seams and smooth imperfections.

match, paying close attention to the seam between the patch and the side of the van (Fig. 5-24).

Once the Bondo has cured, it's a simple matter to finish it off with a "Bondo board" and 80-grit sandpaper. Be sure to use a Bondo board or similar tool so that no "waves" or ripples remain in the Bondo to spoil an otherwise perfect repair. At this point, the repair can be primed, finish-sanded, and "spotted" in to match the existing paint. Or, as we did, the repair can be heavily primed and left for the day the whole van will receive its final finish paint job.

Needless to say, our Chevy looks a whole bunch better with the offending window removed and the hole filled in. This repair method, of course, is not limited just to windows, but can be used on any hole that remains following the removal of a no-longer-wanted piece of equipment, as long as the surrounding metal is not distorted severely. If the side is badly distorted, it'll have to be smoothed out with a hammer and dolly so that the backing panel will mate well and the adhesive will bond as intended. Good luck.

Chapter 6
Flare Fixes

When we first met our camper van, a 1975 Fleetwood "Santana" van conversion, there seemed to be an abundance of room in the stock Dodge fenderwells for just about any wheel/tire combination that we'd want to stuff under them (Fig. 6-1). This opinion had been more or less confirmed by our having never noticed any Dodge vans on the road that had required any sort of surgery in the fenderwell area. "In like Flynn"...or so we thought. Usually, though, the use of that phrase is the "kiss of death," after which nothing ever goes right.

Armed with a brand-new set of Western's Cyclone RV wheels in sizes 8.25 × 6.5 for the front and 9.75 × 16.5 for the rear and Armstrong tires, 10.00 × 16.5 front and 12.00 × 16.5 rear, we drove home to bolt 'em on.

To make a rather long and sorrowful story short, a couple of weeks, two ruined air chisel blades and four lengths of brazing rod later we had our Santana back on the road (Fig. 6-2). But gawd, what a mess in the wheelwell department! Well, at least we had the tire clearance we needed. As far as finishing the opening off was concerned, we had a couple of methods available to us: First, we could hand-fabricate some slinky fender flares from electrical conduit and sheetmetal and be guaranteed that we'd have a one-of-a-kind van, or second, we could install Karvan's trick Mark II flares and skip all the hard work. To show you what's involved we did it both ways.

Fig. 6-1. While plenty adequate for the stock wheel/tire combo, the Dodge fenderwells weren't big enough for the large 10.00 × 16.5s.

KARVAN MARK II

These flares were designed to cure the very problem with which we were faced—massacred fenderwells on late Dodge vans when oversized RV-type tires on wide rims were installed (Fig. 6-3). Thanks to the popularity of 15 in. super-low-profile tires, however, the Mark II flares have not enjoyed the popularity of their pint-sized cousins, the fender-lip flares, because the fenderwells needn't be modified for them to fit. With "standard profile" RV tires like our Armstrongs, however, we couldn't use the smaller flares because, thanks to our air chisel, we no longer had a fender lip to which they could be attached.

Fig. 6-2. With Armstrong tires and Western Cyclone RV wheels in place, openings were trimmed for clearance and welded for strength.

Fig. 6-3. We chose Karvan's big flares because they're the only ones that mount to the body instead of the fenderwell lip.

The Karvan Mark II flares attach to the van's sides instead of the finder lip, allowing up to four inches of body to be trimmed away—enough for the installation of even the largest "floatation" tires for desert off-roading. Thoughtfully, Karvan wrapped the edges of the flares back around so that if 15 in. wheels and tires are used, only a minimum of grungy suspension is allowed to show around the edges of the tire. Through careful design work the flares may be trimmed as necessary for clearance of medium-size (like ours) tires and wheels right on up to the largest sizes without loss of the good looks. Where most trimmed flares *look* like trimmed flares, Karvan Mark IIs look as if they were made that way. Our wheel/tire combination, for instance, forced us to do some pretty heavy trimming—up to two inches in places—of the flares before adequate clearance was gained at full steering lock on full jounce (suspension compressed onto the snubbers). While the photos show that we got pretty heavy with the saber saw, you'd be pretty hard-pressed to find where

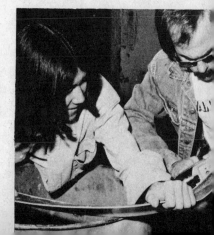

Fig. 6-4. A careful trial fitting showed that some of the front flares needed trimming for tire clearance. A saber saw works well.

Fig. 6-5. With plenty of clearance guaranteed, holes were drilled according to marks on the Karvan flares. Fit was perfect.

we cut now that the installation is complete. Although this may seem like a small point, try it on any other flare you've seen!

While the actual installation of the Mark II flares isn't all that difficult, more care than usual must be exercised to insure that they are positioned properly with respect to the wheels and tires. A fraction of an inch too far forward or rearward will make the whole van look out of proportion—so check, and then double check, to be sure.

A drill, a rivet gun and long shank rivets, a saber saw, a body grinder of some sort, and an able-bodied friend, along with a couple or three hours will handle the installation (Figs. 6-4 through 6-9). Providing, of course, that the welding has been completed.

While we could have left the Karvan flares simply riveted to the van and painted them to match, we decided to go the full route (Fig. 6-10) and mold them to the van's sides for a cleaner, more custom appearance.

Fig. 6-6. The job is much easier if a friend helps hold flare flush to body while rivet gun is used. Use fairly long rivets—it's easier.

Fig. 6-7. Water tank drain spigot caused clearance problems, but these were easily solved with a little saber saw work.

Thanks to Jerry Wesseling at Old Glory Vans, the job of finishing the flares was completed in short order. Jerry, owner of the well known red, white, and blue van *Old Glory*, and his ace body man, Darrell Keen, wheeled our van into the work area behind the ultradifferent (would you believe hanging plants, rock music, and a 'fridge full of cool ones for the customers?) shop and started jammin' on our truck.

PRELIMINARIES

The first step, and one of the most important, is to carefully grind the paint from the sides of the van surrounding

Fig. 6-8. The cutout will look better after molding.

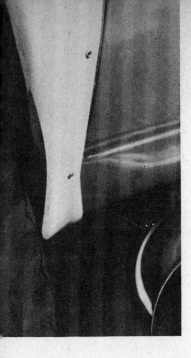

Fig. 6-9. Only the front edges of the rear flares needed to be trimmed, and then only slightly and easily disguised.

the flares for a distance of six to eight inches, depending on the amount of molding necessary for a smooth, finished product (Fig. 6-11). At the same time, the gel coat on the flares should be lightly ground to provide a tooth to which the plastic filler material may bond. A coarse-grit disc is used for the van's sides and the flares themselves. Darrell chamfered the edges of the flares to provide a smoother blend requiring less filler. This process should be done with great care to save work in the later stages.

Fig. 6-10. Chamfering the edges at this point will make the molding-in work just that much easier. We used an air grinder for speed.

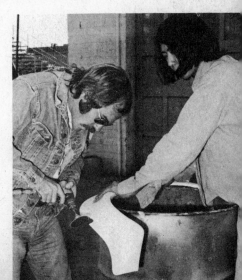

Fig. 6-11. Using a coarse-grit disc, grind the paint from the area around the flares. Scuff the flares at the same time.

With the surfaces prepared in this manner, the plastic filler is mixed according to the manufacturer's directions and applied, doing one flare at a time, to approximate the finished shape as closely as possible (Fig. 6-12). Plastic filler should not be applied too thickly at one time. Two or three thinner coats will be much stronger and much easier to work.

SHAPING

When the filler has *kicked-off* but not yet hardened thoroughly—experience is the best teacher when determining the proper degree of hardness—a half-round "cheese grater" tool is used to rough-shape the contours (Fig. 6-13). Using this auto supply store tool, the curves and angles necessary for a smooth, finished job may be quickly formed without the ripples and waves that occur when sandpaper is used. A linoleum knife is handy to remove filler from door edges and seams. Usually, a few low spots will remain after rough-shaping the contours with the grater, requiring the application of a second coat of filler. Be sure that *all* surfaces to which the filler is applied, including all parts of the previous coat, are thoroughly scuffed with coarse-grit sandpaper before the second coat of filler is applied. Failure to do this may cause a poor bond between the first and second coats.

Fig. 6-12. Bondo is then applied to the seam with applicator. Make it as smooth as possible to save work later.

Fig. 6-13. A half-round "cheese grater" shaping tool makes short work of the excess. Use before Bondo sets up too hard.

The second coat (and third, should it be necessary) of plastic filler should also be carefully shaped using the grater and knife until the transition from flare to van side is smooth and free of ripples and bumps. Once the shape has been roughed out, a combination of tools including a hand or power "Bondo board," sanding block, and a small disc grinder may be used to further shape the filler and smooth the transition from flare to side (Figs. 6-14 through 6-16). Coarse-grit sandpaper, 36- or 80-grit paper, should be used for this purpose. Once the whole flare is as smooth as you can make it with the rough-grit paper, sand with progressively finer grits until everything is as smooth as possible using 220-grit wet-and-dry paper. Small imperfections that still remain may be filled with spot putty or a small dab of plastic filler.

FINISHING

Once the flare is smooth and sanded with 220 sandpaper, you're ready to shoot on a heavy coat of primer, either enamel or lacquer depending on the type of paint you'll use to finish your van (Fig. 6-17). Further sanding should be left until you're ready to shoot the final gloss coats.

Fig. 6-14. Tight curves such as those of the fenderwell accent lines are best shaped with a small grinder disc.

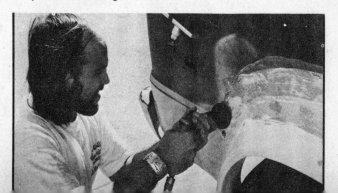

There, even though your arms are sore and your driveway is littered with plastic shavings, dust and used-up sandpaper, it wasn't as bad as you figured, right? Until, that is, you remember that you've still got three more flares to go!

CAPTIONS FOR FOLLOWING 8-PAGE COLOR SECTION

Plate 1. Flying Eagle II, a modern day cruiser, keeps a sharp lookout ahead, so don't be surprised if she suddenly passes you.

Plate 2. Rest comfortably under the wings of the Eagle while enjoying the luxury of rich wood bulkheads and a light grained ceiling.

Plate 3. Step through the louvered door to check a falling barometer and, perhaps, to rest up for the coming storm.

Plate 4. Ride with Rainbow Rider and maybe you'll find the pot of gold—but look sharp for it may be closer than you think.

Plate 5. Sink into a chair, plop on the headphones, and enjoy the warmth radiated by this comfortable abode.

Plate 6. The orange brilliance of this decor will always stand out under the light streaming through the rear window and skylight.

Plate 7. Step into Massage Parlor for a trip you'll never forget. Note the wrought iron rack for lashing down luggage on a long trip.

Plate 8. Imagine those long, slender fingers easing weary muscles as you relax into the folds of this deeply cushioned haven.

Plate 9. With a full bank of lights up front and huge pipes out the sides, this van waits to roar through the night air.

Plate 10. Snuggle up to the warmth of this plush setting and partake of the spirits—just to ward off a chill from the damp night air, you understand.

Fig. 6-17. A heavy coat of primer and flares are ready for finish-sanding and paint. Plan on a full day's work.

METAL FLARES

"Glass is," as they say, "class." "But steel is real"—and if you run an older van, you don't have much choice in the matter. Fiberglass manufacturers are concentrating on the late-model van market, leaving the early van owner with the choice of steel flares or skinny tires.

True, installing metal flares is harder than pop-riveting fiberglass units and therefore somewhat more expensive. However, metal flares do have the inherent advantage of being stronger and more able to withstand minor shunts without breaking. To see how metal flares are fashioned, we went to Customs by Eddie Paul, El Segundo, CA, and watched while a Chevy van received the treatment.

The first step is to determine the front contour of the flare. Measure the length of the flare and the distance from the stock fender to the outer edge of the mounted tire (Fig. 6-18). Using these measurements, trace the flare's form on a piece of paper and cut out a template (Fig. 6-19). The same procedure is followed for shaping the flare's rear section.

Fig. 6-18. The front section of the fender is measured to determine the contour of the flare.

Fig. 6-19. These measurements are then transferred to a piece of paper and a template is cut.

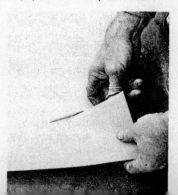

Fig. 6-20. Using chalk, the outline of the template is marked on a 16-gauge trailer fender. The identical procedure is followed for the rear section of the flare.

Place the paper template over a 16-gauge fender from a trailer, outline in chalk, and cut along the line (Fig. 6-20 and 6-21). The rough cut flare section is then ground smooth and tack-welded to the body (Fig. 6-22). Again, the same process is used for the flare's rear piece (Fig. 6-23). With both front and

Fig. 6-21. Both front and rear flare sections are then cut out of the trailer fender.

Fig. 6-22. While holding the flare section along the leading edge of the stock fender, it is tack-welded in place.

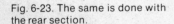

Fig. 6-23. The same is done with the rear section.

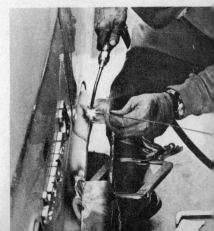

Fig. 6-24. The center section is now measured and cut from 16-gauge flat sheetmetal and curled to match the outer edge of the other pieces.

rear sections secured, the center gap is filled by cutting a piece of 16-gauge metal to fit, curling the outer edge to match the rest of the flare, and tack-welding it (Figs. 6-24 and 6-25).

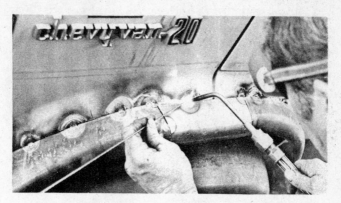

Fig. 6-25. It, too, is then tack-welded to the body of the van.

Another paper template is made for the lower front section of the flare. It, too, is cut from a piece of flat 16-gauge metal, contoured to fit the shape of the flare, and tack-welded to the

Fig. 6-26. A template is also measured and cut for the lower front section of the flare. This piece is then contoured and welded in place.

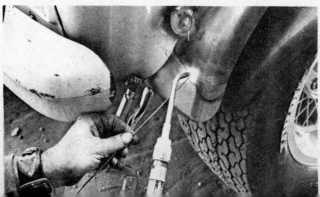

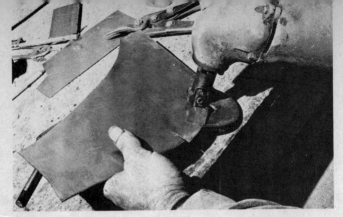

Fig. 6-27. After shaping and cutting the lower rear section, the outside corner is notched.

van (Fig. 6-26). For the lower-rear section a template is also needed. Once the metal is cut, the outside corner is notched so it can be curled under to provide structural strength (Figs. 6-27

Fig. 6-28. The outer edge and notched corner are then curled under, not only to match the rest of the flare, but to provide structural strength as well.

and 6-28). These notches are then welded up and the piece is attached to the body (Figs. 6-29 and 6-30). At this point the open seams are welded shut and the basic flare is completed (Figs. 6-31 and 6-32).

Fig. 6-29. The notches are then welded up and ground smooth.

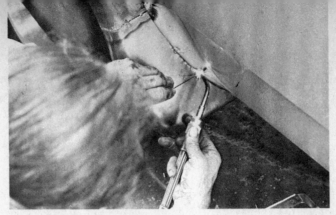

Fig. 6-30. The lower rear section is now tack-welded in place.

Fig. 6-31. The small gap in the stock fender is filled with a plug and welded shut. If Bondo were used instead, it would repeatedly crack—creating the need for almost constant repair.

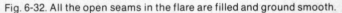

Fig. 6-32. All the open seams in the flare are filled and ground smooth.

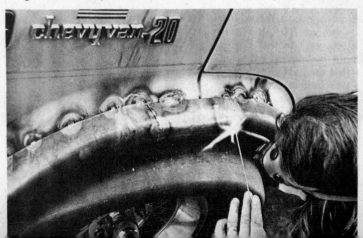

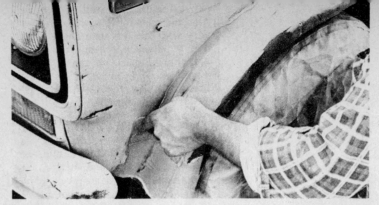

Fig. 6-33. Several coats of Bondo are applied and repeatedly sanded before the flare is primered and readied for the finishing paint job.

The welds are now ground down and the flare's exposed edges smoothed. Several coats of Bondo are applied to cover the welds. After smoothing and sanding the Bondo, the flare is primed and readied for the finishing coat of paint (Fig. 6-33).

Due to the amount of measuring, cutting, grinding and welding, this is not your normal everyday backyard project (Fig. 6-34). However, Customs by Eddie Paul is about to make it somewhat simpler by marketing pre-cut and ground (ready-to-weld) flare kits. It still may not be as easy as pop-riveting glass flares, but if you have an early-model van, what is your alternative?

Fig. 6-34. A lot of work, but the results are worth it.

Chapter 7

Three
For The Top

Once upon a time van roofs were considered to be the dullest part of a van—something to keep the rain out. But no more. Now vanners are discovering two very good looking—and useful—roof fixtures: wings and roof racks.

ROOF RACK

When we decided to add a roof rack to give us some extra storage space, we wanted something that was nice looking, yet still well-designed and well-built.

We found the answer with a gold-anodized rack and ladder combination from Top Line Manufacturing (Fig. 7-1). The gold color would look super with the dark metallic green of our Dodge and the extra touch of the Dodge emblems cut into the supports of the rack was just what we were looking for in the way of something extra.

The roof racks are offered in both three-rail and four-rail styles. The four-rail offers a closed, box-shaped rail enclosure, while the three-rail style is open at the front end. We chose the three-rail style, which is four feet wide and five feet long.

With the help of the folks at Top Line, we bolted on the whole affair, both rack and ladder, in a short time, once we solved one troublesome problem.

The first step is to mount the ladder to the rear of the van. While the ladder and rack are offered separately, there seems to be little use to the rack without a ladder to offer accessibility to the roof.

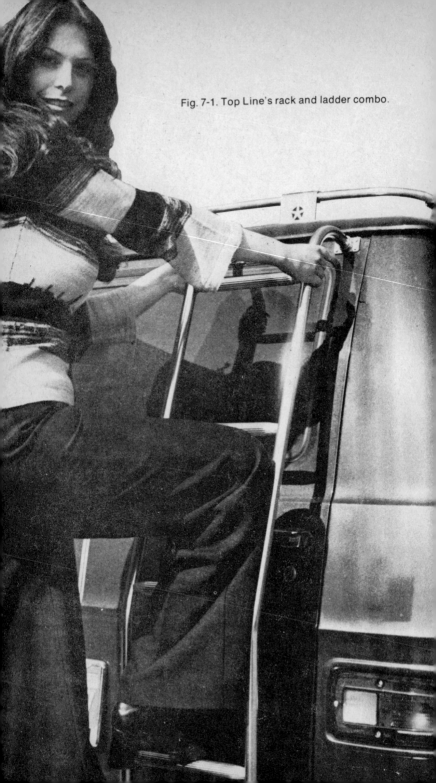

Fig. 7-1. Top Line's rack and ladder combo.

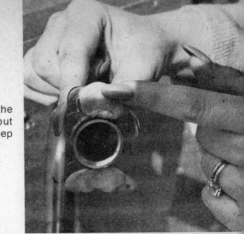

Fig. 7-2. When mounting the ladder, putty tape is first put behind screw holes to keep water out and prevent rust.

The ladder goes on first for an obvious reason. Once the ladder is on, it makes the roof installation much easier.

The Top Line ladder mounts directly to the door of the Dodge. Thus it swings out with the door when the door is opened and presents no loading problems. We just have to remember when backing up that the ladder does stick out a touch farther than the bumper.

Four brackets on the ladder supports are held to the door with self-tapping screws. The work will go quicker if you drill pilot holes before inserting the screws, and you will need someone to help hold the ladder while you drill. Before bolting down the ladder, be sure to place a quantity of putty tape behind the screw holes of the brackets (Fig. 7-2). As the screws are tightened down, the putty will be drawn in and seal the hole, thus preventing water from leaking in and starting rust (Figs. 7-3 and 7-4).

Fig. 7-3. Installing the ladder, which comes completely assembled, takes two people. One holds the ladder in place, while the other puts in the screws.

While the rack can be assembled up on the roof, we recommend laying it out on the ground and connecting all the pieces as shown on the diagram on the box. The rack comes in seven pieces (Figs. 7-5 through 7-7): the two side rails, the end rail, two bars that connect the sides of the end rail, and two end pieces for the open ends of the rack.

Where we ran into a problem was when we accidentally put the pieces which join the side rails to the end rail in the wrong way. While this may sound odd, the distance from the bend to one end of the curved joining piece is shorter than the distance to the other end.

The easy way to know if you have connected everything up properly is to measure the distance between the side rails in several spots. If it is four feet, you're all set. If not, try again.

Now the end pieces are placed into the ends of the side rails to provide a nice, finished appearance. Then the small set screws which hold the various pieces together are tightened and you're ready to mount the rack to the roof (Fig. 7-8). Just don't forget the putty tape behind the screw holes of the brackets (Fig. 7-9). Now drill the self-tapping screws supplied with the kit into place and you're finished (Figs. 7-10 and 7-11).

The whole operation should take you less than an hour and the resulting improved appearance is certainly worth the time invested.

By the way, the ladder is perfectly capable of holding almost anyone. It is well-constructed and one 180-pounder clambered all over it several times, tugging and pulling, and found it capable of taking any reasonable load.

114

Fig. 7-5. All the pieces for the Top Line roof rack, including the self-tapping screws for mounting, are neatly packed in the box.

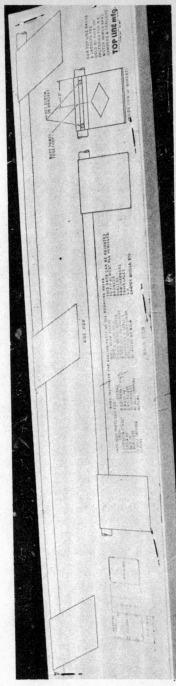

Fig. 7-6. Complete instructions for assembly and mounting are printed right on the box.

Fig. 7-7. It is easiest to put the rack together on the ground, before bringing the whole assembly to the roof of the van.

ADJUSTABLE WINGS

One of the most popular west coast van modifications is the installation of a "wing," *a la* race car style, on the rear of the top (Figs. 7-12 and 7-13). Not only do the race-bred devices look great, but they also offer some very real advantages.

Offered by several manufacturers, wings are designed to deflect air moving across the van's top upward, thus creating a downward force on the van itself. This downward force,

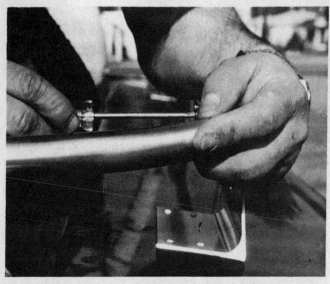

Fig. 7-8. When everything is in place, tighten the set screws that hold the curved section which connects the rear rail to the side rails. Screws which hold end pieces should also be tightened at this time.

116

Fig. 7-9. Putty tape should be also be used behind the screw holes of the roof rack.

which varies with vehicle speed—the faster the speed, the more downward force created—in effect makes the van heavier and thus creates more traction on the rear wheels. Since most vans have a marked weight bias to the front, this added rear weight can be very beneficial to the van's handling capabilities at speed.

There is, as road racers well know, a definite drawback to wings, however. This major disadvantage is a very significant increase in vehicle drag—its resistance to moving through the air—caused by both the wing's frontal area and the air turbulence it creates. Because vans are high-drag vehicles to

Fig. 7-10. Once up top, make sure the rack is lined up straight, and that there are no obstructions.

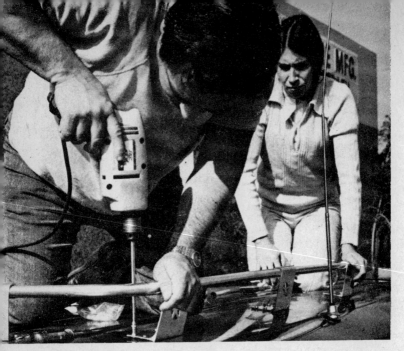

Fig. 7-11. The final step is to put self-tapping screws in the roof rack brackets.

begin with, additional drag caused by the wing is very likely to further reduce already low highway gas mileage. Racers get around this additional drag factor by constructing their wings so that they may be adjusted, or trimmed, from within the car. When straightaways are encountered, the wing's wind resistance is reduced by trimming it for minimum drag. On corners, where traction is important, the wing is trimmed to provide maximum downward force and, at the same time, maximum drag to help slow the car without the use of the brakes.

Fig. 7-12. Bob Unkefer (Varmint) of Liberty, Missouri, and member of Vans Am and NSRA's National Van Division Director got the urge for a wing on his van recently. After careful measuring, necessary holes were marked and drilled.

Fig. 7-13. Hardware supplied with the American Racing Equipment wing was of the highest quality and included rubber grommets to insure against leakage and a spoiled headliner. Square shouldered bolts make for one-man installation.

On vans, as on any other vehicle, the steeper the angle of the wing, the greater the wind resistance, or drag, it creates (Figs. 7-14 and 7-15). So, to minimize drag, the wing should be mounted to the rear of the van and trimmed as close to parallel with the top of the van as possible. The all-around optimum

Fig. 7-14. Tipping the leading edge steeply downward is a very common trend but can increase drag by up to 50 percent and reduce already-low gas mileage. This position, though, creates the greatest traction increase at speed.

position, then, would be a *slight* downward front tilt so as to take advantage of increased traction at highway speeds while minimizing excess drag (Fig. 7-16).

In short, wings are great accessories for vans, adding both good looks and additional highway stability (Fig. 7-17). An

Fig. 7-15. Tipping the leading edge too far upward not only looks ridiculous but has adverse effect on both drag and traction at highway speeds. Race applications of wings are often able to be trimmed from inside car.

Fig. 7-16. Slight downward tilt seems to be the best compromise position, giving increased traction at higher speeds while not creating too much drag. Not surprisingly, this position is also the one that looks the best.

improper mounting angle, however, can increase vehicle drag by as much as 50 percent and noticeably reduce highway mileage. The best part, though, is that they're relatively inexpensive and easy to install, as the accompanying step-by-step photos show.

FIXED WINGS

Something new has been popping up on the tops of vans. Adjustable wings, usually made of aluminum and patterned after wings used on race cars, are great for the mechanical minded, but do not have the flash of fiberglass fixed wings.

In the last few months more and more wings have been appearing with a new look, one more suited to the overall shape of the van. Giving an appearance that has been called by some the "Trans-Am look," the new wing stretches the full width of the van. The ends of the wing gently curve down to form the supports, which are attached to the roof at the sides of the van.

The first model to be mass-produced by any manufacturer that we know of is coming from Imaginary Glass (Fig. 7-18). We visited their plant in Anaheim, California, to take a look at their Nor-Cal Wing so we could pick up some installation tips and judge for ourselves just how well the wing is put together.

Fig. 7-17. Wings are commonly available in both aluminum and fiberglass. While glass wings may be painted, the aluminum units like Bob's may be left uncoated, clear-epoxied to reduce maintenance, or even anodized to match van.

Quality is something that Imaginary Glass products are known for, and their wing is no exception. It took three years of designing and working with various prototypes before the final production model was produced. Though their first attempts met with failure, they kept going and now they have a wing that is good looking, easy to install and made to last under the stress of being pulled through the air at 55 mph.

The upper section of the wing has been specially strengthened to withstand wind pressure without bending or breaking. The extra strength also prevents another problem. Early models had shown a tendency to sag in the middle after several weeks of use.

The supporting legs of the wing have a steel plate imbedded in the bottom. This provides an area so that self-tapping screws have something solid to grip when the

Fig. 7-18. Imaginary Glass' new wing looks good from any angle.

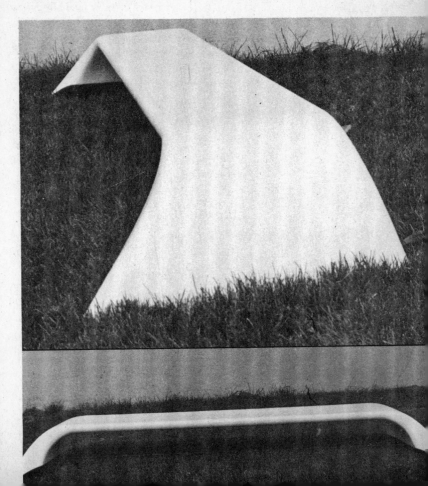

Fig. 7-19. First, putty tape is laid on the base of the wing. Use double thickness to assure a good, leak-proof fit.

wing is mounted. When correctly in place, the wing holds so well you can shake the van by the wing all day without dislodging it.

The first few wings produced were all finished in a white gel coat. But since van owners will be painting the wings to match their vehicles, wings are now being finished in primer. This saves the buyer the trouble of priming before painting.

Fig. 7-20. The next step is to line up the wing and check for straightness.

Fig. 7-21. If wing is mounted just slightly above rain gutter, it won't interfere with the function of the gutter.

One hint, be sure the wing is completely painted before it is installed. Once in place, the underside will be impossible to paint with any type of spray gun.

The wing has been designed for both fit and style. In addition to having the proper curve in the base to get a proper fit, each model wing is also made so that the body curve of the particular model van is matched by the curve of the wing!

To show how much confidence the makers have in their wing, Imaginary Glass has a 100-percent guarantee against defects from the manufacturer. They also guarantee the fit of their wing.

Fig. 7-22. Before drilling any holes, look closely at this picture. Dotted lines show location of steel plate in bottom of support leg of wing. Screws must be drilled through this plate to hold the wing securely.

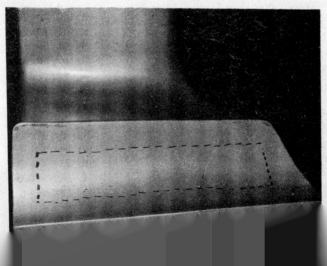

Fig. 7-23. Line up carefully, make sure you're drilling into the steel plate in the wing, then drill and insert screws. A partner to hold down the wing helps.

Now, exactly how is a wing like this mounted correctly? The procedure isn't difficult and takes only an hour or two, but there are a couple of important points in the installation process. We watched Corky Melhuish of Custom Specialties put one on a Dodge.

First, take the wing and put two layers of silicone putty tape (the kind often used for the installation of sunroofs) around the base of the wing supports (Fig. 7-19). This will seal the bottom of the wing and prevent water from leaking in and causing the mounting screws to rust.

Next, line up the wing so it is where you want it on the back of the van, lined up straight (Fig. 7-20). On the Dodge it was easy, since we could line up on the body line. The base of the wing is curved to fit the curve of the roof and thus can be mounted flush with the roof gutter.

Corky, however, recommends that the wing be mounted slightly above the gutter. This way there won't be any interference with the normal functioning of the gutter (Fig. 7-21).

If you have already installed a headliner, it now should be removed. The wing can be mounted from the top of the van, but to keep a sanitary look, we suggest you mount it from the inside out.

Fig. 7-24. This is how it should look from the inside when you're done. Five screws should ensure that the wing will stay in place.

Five self-tapping screws can now be drilled through the roof from the inside and into the base of the wing support leg (Figs. 7-22 through 7-24). Now switch sides and put five more screws into the other supporting leg of the wing. Don't forget the metal plates. They are located in the center of the base, and if the screws miss the plates, they won't hold the wing correctly. Check the accompanying photos to see exactly where the plate is located in the wing supports.

All that's left at this point is the cleanup work. Using a small stepladder so you can see what you're doing, strip off the excess putty tape where the wing meets the roof outside (Fig. 7-25). Replace the headliner inside and you're done (Fig. 7-26).

Fig. 7-25. After the wing is installed, clean putty left sticking out from base of wing.

Fig. 7-26. The end result. Wing design carries out the curves of the van body.

If you don't even have a headliner to worry about, the job should take you less than an hour. With a headliner, the time the job takes will depend on how hard the headliner is to remove and replace, but in any case, you should be able to do the deed in an easy Sunday afternoon.

Chapter 8
Paint Your
Van Like A Pro

This chapter takes you from basic Bondo and monocolor paint to the ultimate in custom paint—pearlescent flame. Read on.

At this stage the body is in pretty fair shape and we can concentrate on the small stuff that makes the difference between a good and great paint job. Read the captions carefully, because they reveal some of the tricks that have made Emmett Glasgow of Street Customs Limited one of the most respected painters in the trade.

Once the color coat is on, you can rest easy with a stage 1 professional paint job. Or, you can elect to go on to stage 2, 3, and as far as your imagination will take you.

And even if you don't want to take paint gun in hand and do battle with your pride and joy, it is helpful to learn what is involved in serious, state-of-art custom painting.

THE BASICS

In order to learn more about custom van painting techniques, we visited Mike Love of Custom Paint Specialties, in Riverside, California. Mike, well-known for his wildly flamed black '65 Olds 442, has been custom painting vans for several years now and started in his front yard! Since that time Mike has acquired a shop and is much in demand by individual vanners and by area van dealers. In fact, Mike and his assistant, Terry, have been flown by dealers to many other parts of the country to ply their trade on eastern vans! When we learned that Mike had painted nearly 1500 vans in his

Fig. 8-1. The original bronze with butterscotch mid-band stripe was a little too RV-ish for a custom van and, besides, it was well primer-spotted thanks to the installation of Karvan flares and smoothing of the hood. The first step was to wash the van down with PrepSol.

Fig. 8-2. The next step was a light machine sanding with 320-grit discs to scuff the original surface for better paint adhesion. This operation also causes any flaws in the van's surface to become immediately apparent for future repair.

Fig. 8-3. Thanks to the many recreational vehicle safety laws, our Santana conversion was dotted with many aluminum warning plaques which were blind-riveted in place. For appearance's sake, these were removed by drilling out the rivets and filling the holes with braze.

Fig. 8-4. The slight ripples and imperfections that remained after the removal of both warning tags and factory trim required a thin skim of body filler. Any small indentations that require attention should also be repaired at this time. Be sure the surface is clean for Bondo.

Fig. 8-5. Once the body filler has hardened, the spots may be smoothed with a medium-grit disc sander or with a sanding block. Surface should be roughed into shape with sander and finished by hand using sanding block or a Bondo board. Some spots may require a second coat of filler.

Fig. 8-6. Areas repaired with body filler should receive a heavy coat of primer to fill the rough sanding marks. Use primer as thick as possible at this stage to fill minor imperfectons with only one or two applications.

Fig. 8-7. With repaired areas semi-finished, attention may be turned to hand-sanding the areas inaccessible to the power sander. Depending on surface condition, either 220 or 320 wet-or-dry paper may be used. Use great care around chrome or tape it off first to prevent scratches.

Fig. 8-8. Blending flares into the surrounding areas is slow, time-consuming work and should be done with great care for smooth, finished products. Now is the time, also, to sand the often rock-chipped areas on the lower body including rocker panels and fender lips. Take your time.

Fig. 8-9. Slight body ripples, too, should receive careful attention at this stage. A light hand, a body hammer and paddle, grinder and body filler, along with a great deal of patience will usually set things straight. Large ripples, though, should probably be left to the pros.

Fig. 8-10. It is important that every surface to receive new paint be sanded or scuffed with 320 to allow the new surface to bond with the old surface properly. Door and hood edges, fresh-air louvers often are overlooked, resulting in the new paint flaking, exposing the old color underneath.

Fig. 8-11. Once the entire van has been sanded and the repaired areas semi-finished and primed, it's time to ready the van for the first coat of primer. Wheel covers like these are handy, but newspaper will work OK, too. Brown wrapping paper, though, is best.

Fig. 8-12. All trim that is not to be removed should be carefully taped before the first coat of primer is applied. Remember, it's easier to scrape paint off chrome than it is to touch up areas not painted. Be sure to buy your tape from an automotive paint supply store!

Fig. 8-13. A heavy coat of primer/surfacer is then applied to repaired areas. Lacquer primer can usually be used over lacquer paint, factory paint, and sometimes over well-cured enamel. If in doubt (assuming final paint will be enamel), use enamel primer. Or, try a small test area.

Fig. 8-14. Using 220-grit wet-or-dry paper, the heavily primed areas should be sanded with a sanding block where possible, and by hand for curved areas. Pinholes, sanding marks and slight imperfections will still remain at this point, but major imperfections should be absent.

career with nearly zero come-backs, we knew that we were in the hands of a true expert.

When we asked Mike to give us a demonstration of his artistry and perhaps pass along a few of his tricks, he began by explaining that preparation of the surface to be painted is of utmost importance to the success of the job. "I work mostly on new or freshly painted vans now," Mike explained, "so I usually have a good surface on which to paint when the vans

Fig. 8-15. Areas such as door jambs, hood edges, rocker panels, scoop edges should be detail-sanded at this time as well. If they're not to receive paint, they should be carefully taped off to prevent overspray from settling on them. Take your time here for a truly professional job.

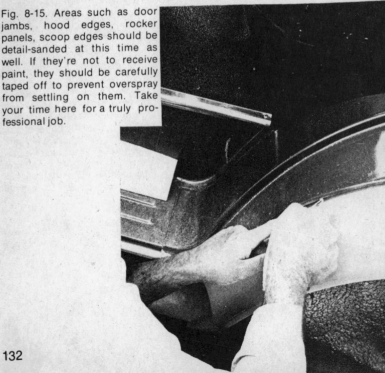

Fig. 8-16. Curved and hard-to-get-at areas must be carefully hand-sanded. There's no substitute for experience in this area, but remember that tiny ripples can be felt easily even though they're too small to be seen. Always try for smooth curves and rounded edges.

come in. Guys with seasoned paint jobs should be extra careful in the preparation steps. After all, custom paint is designed to enhance good paint jobs, not to hide bad ones.''

The first step in preparing for custom paint is a thorough wash with soap and water followed by a good rinse. Once dry, the van should be wiped down with a rag soaked in DuPont PrepSol, allowed to set for a few seconds, and then wiped with

Fig. 8-17. Preliminary sanding will expose bare metal and Bondo in many spots where surface isn't yet smooth. A second heavy priming is usually necessary to further protect the surface. All areas should again be primed, though coat can be lighter in perfectly smooth areas.

Fig. 8-18. Assuming the top needs no repair, it may now be sanded with 320-grit paper just like the lower body for good paint adhesion.

Fig. 8-19. The second primer coat should be attacked with 320-grit wet-or-dry paper, working to perfect the surface and improve the blend where body was repaired or modified. A block is helpful on large, flat areas but this step should be done by hand on curved surfaces.

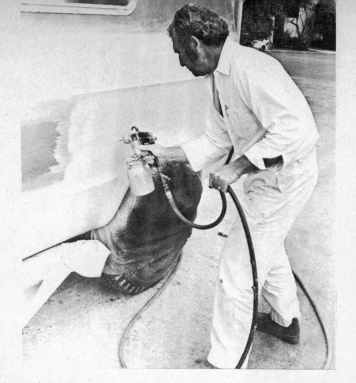

Fig. 8-20. Assuming that all problem areas have been conquered to your satisfaction in the previous steps, you can now give the van a generous once-over with primer thinned according to instructions.

Fig. 8-21. Don't forget to allow yourself access to the vehicle by leaving the door handle button untaped until the last moment. This is a good time, too, to check items previously taped for flaws.

Fig. 8-22. Spot putty may now be used to fill the minor flaws and pinholes too small to fill with body filler. Use spot putty extremely thin or it'll cause problems later. Application may be done with a rubber squeegee.

Fig. 8-23. Very minor dings or chips in the underlying paint that went unnoticed previously may be filled with spot putty using a razor blade as a squeegee. This method serves to apply putty exactly level with the surrounding surface.

Fig. 8-24. Sanding in areas that cannot be block sanded should be done with folded sandpaper, fingers together with pressure applied lightly over entire finger area. Do not sand with only one or two fingers, nor should pressure be greatest at second knuckle; leads to marks easily visible later.

Fig. 8-25. All edges like those around doors, fenderwells and trim should be very carefully sanded until immaculately smooth for good paint adhesion as well as for good finished appearance. Nothing looks worse than a smoothly painted ragged edge.

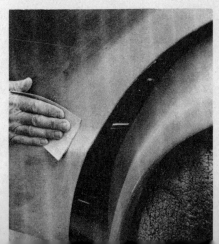

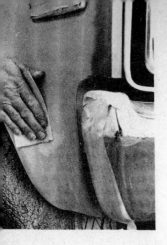

Fig. 8-26. Spot puttied areas should be finish-sanded carefully with light, smooth touch—being careful to prevent sandpaper from loading up. Extra care used in curved areas such as this pays excellent dividends on the finished product. Beware of large waves, especially.

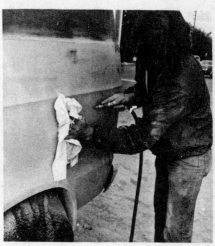

Fig. 8-27. Blow the dust away from work areas frequently and examine progress. The 320 paper you've been using leaves a satin finish that, when viewed carefully, will expose any flaws much like the glossy finished paint. Take your time and get it right the first time.

Fig. 8-28. Once you're satisfied that the van is as perfectly smooth and straight as you can make it, blow it off with compressed air and move it into the paint booth. Areas to receive tape may need a degreasing with ammonia and water to allow tape to stick well.

Fig. 8-29. Final taping of windows, sidepipes, tires, etc., may now be done. Use great care when taping to make sure folds do not occur that may trap dust that'll later emerge to ruin all your hard work. Kraft paper works best, though double layers of newspaper will work OK.

a clean and dry cloth (Fig. 8-36). This will remove most of the built-up wax and any fingerprints, grease or oil that would spoil the paint adhesion.

Mike then lays out his design using 1/4 in. 3M masking tape (Fig. 8-37). He uses the highest quality of tape available (3M is a good one) regardless of its price, as cheap tape won't "work" as well as the good stuff and often leaves an adhesive film that must be cleaned off later. As Mike puts it, the design

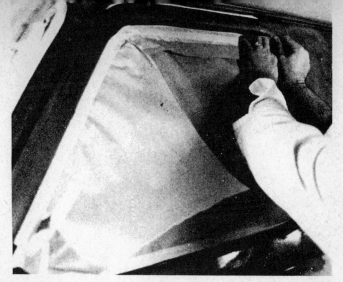

Fig. 8-30. The areas around the windows are the trickiest, so take your time—as they're also the areas most noticeable on the finished product. Don't forget to tape the weatherstripping around all doors as the paint will work its way into the cracks. If not to be painted, tape off doorjambs, too.

should follow the general lines of the van and blend well with the van's natural curves. This is where a professional's skill puts him a couple of steps ahead of the do-it-yourself vanner. "How do I do it?" asked Mike. "Well, I guess it's mostly experience. Because every van I do is different—and I've done

Fig. 8-31. If you can't or don't want to remove all the little trim goodies—it's best if they're taken off—1/8 in. or 1/4 in. masking tape may be used to protect them. It's available at automotive paint/supply stores. This job is slow and laborious at best, but take your time.

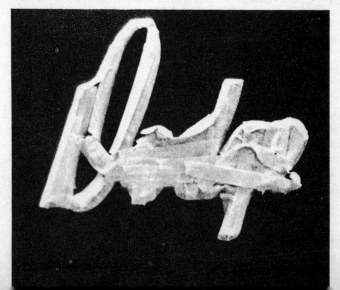

Fig. 8-32. The final blow-off with compressed air should be accompanied by a thorough rub-down with a soft, lint-free cloth. This loosens any stubborn dust particles while also helping anchor tape even more securely. Follow this with a PrepSol bath and a thorough wipedown with a tack rag—twice!

a lot of them—I think I've made every mistake there is to be made and learned from them all."

Mike uses 3M masking paper as well as tape because, as he jokingly puts it, "it don't leak." Other material such as kraft paper or even newspaper can be used to mask the van, but must be used in several layers to prevent leakage. Once the van is masked in the desired design, Mike and Terry use 3M General Purpose Pads, stock number 7447, to scuff the paint next to the tape (Fig. 8-38). The pads are used instead of sandpaper because, in addition to scuffing the paint, they also help stick the edges of the tape down securely so that the paint won't "creep" underneath and thus spoil the nice, crisp edge when the tape is removed. Once the edges are well scuffed, the

Fig. 8-33. The painter's stance, called the Glasgow Crouch, is also essential to the success of your paint job. Seriously, paint should be applied from the top down on each coat, working from panel to panel with long strokes parallel to the panel's surface. From three to four coats will likely be necessary for a smooth finished job, with just enough time allowed between coats for the paint to begin to get tacky. This, and the amount of paint to apply with each coat, are largely a matter of experience when it comes to enamel. Lacquer, on the other hand, should be applied slightly wet for each coat with the final coat quite wet for smoothness to ease wet-sanding chores later on. If you possibly can, spend a day or so practicing on a spare door or two to perfect your technique, especially with enamel.

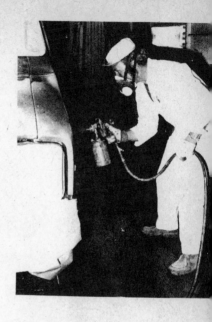

remainder of the panel is sanded with 3M wet/dry paper, 320 grit, dry (Fig. 8-39). The gloss of the original paint must be completely broken by the sanding or the paint that follows will not stick. Once sanded, the panels are blown off with an air

Fig. 8-34. Emmett Glasgow used Sherwin-Williams KEM Transport Enamel for our van, mixed strictly according to manufacturer's instructions along with the recommended catalyst. If you're new to the paint game, consult the paint manufacturer's representative before buying or applying your paint. He is the expert on his product and is aware of local conditions that will very likely affect the application of the final paint. He may be contacted through your automotive paint-supply store and will be more than happy to help you with your choice of paint and its proper application. Just don't forget to follow his advice—to the letter.

hose and wiped again with PrepSol to remove any remaining wax, grease and fingerprints (Figs. 8-40 and 8-41).

Being certain that the PrepSol has thoroughly evaporated after being wiped off, Mike then lightly shoots the panels with

Fig. 8-35. With all coats applied, including the final coat which was mixed with just a hint of pearl for luster, our van sits ready for the overnight drying period.

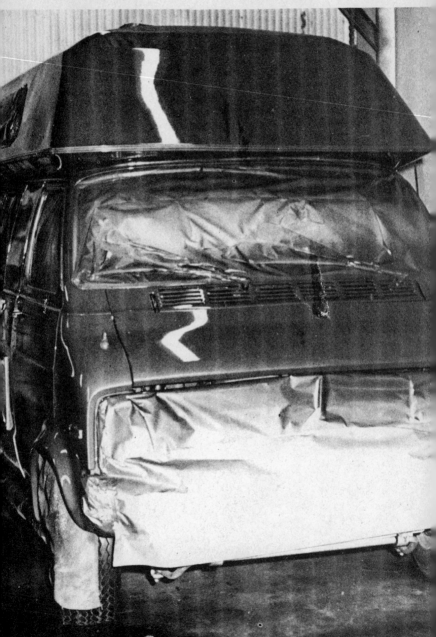

Fig. 8-36. Following a thorough wash and wipe with PrepSol, Mike lays out the pattern with 1/4 in. masking tape. Design should follow lines of van and complement them. Experience like Mike's is invaluable here.

Fig. 8-37. Once design is laid out, Terry goes about the tedious job of masking off the rest of the van to prevent overspray from marring base finish. Use of good quality masking tape and paper is secret of quick, good job.

Fig. 8-38. Close-up of scuffing operation with General Purpose Pads shows that tape edge is crisp and neat. Gloss of original paint must be broken for proper adhesion of the custom paint. Use care and patience here.

Fig. 8-39. Large areas such as the inner design surfaces may be scuffed using 320 wet/dry paper dry. Keep sandpaper away from the tape edges as the sandpaper—unlike the pads—will tend to shred the masking tape.

Fig. 8-40. Once the sanding operation is complete, blow off the entire surface with high-pressure air to eliminate dust and sanding residue. Pay special attention to trim holes and paper folds where dust accumulates.

Fig. 8-41. A good wipe-down with DuPont PrepSol follows to remove any remaining wax, grease and fingerprints that would, if allowed to remain, cause paint to discolor or lift at a later date. Wipe off with clean cloth.

Fig. 8-42. Mike uses Ditzler DL-1970 sealer on all areas that are to receive custom paint. The sealer prevents any possible reaction between the new and the old paint and also prevents any color "bleed" that would ruin job.

Ditzler DL-1970 sealer, which is allowed to dry for about 15 minutes before he continues with the next step (Fig. 8-42). Once the sealer has dried, Mike shoots the entire panel with Ditzler DMA-311 white acrylic lacquer as a base coat. The white is sprayed in three fairly light coats and allowed to "flash" dry between coats. The third coat is applied slightly wet and then allowed to dry for about a half-hour.

ACCENT LINES

Following the drying period, accent lines which will appear white in the finished product are laid out within the

Fig. 8-43. After the white acrylic lacquer base coat has been applied, Mike adds 1/8 in. tape to accent panel. Area where tape is applied will appear white, like the base coat, on the finished product—for added emphasis.

145

Fig. 8-44. A portion of the upper panel is taped off now and will be the area used for the mural. White base coat is a must under both pattern and mural areas for transparent colors to work correctly.

panel to contrast with the finished pattern. As a little trick, Mike explained that 1/8 in. masking tape may be applied to the extreme outside edge of the panel at this time so that, when the tape is removed, it will appear that the design has been striped in white around the edges (Fig. 8-43). Clever, right? Then the mural area is masked (Fig. 8-44).

SMOKING

The customer wanted his panels to feature one of Mike's unique techniques, a smoked effect that appears three-dimensional under the finish tints. To accomplish this neat effect, Mike fires up his trusty torch with acetylene only and carefully adjusts it with the regulator set at about 13 psi, so that it just barely smokes (Fig. 8-45).

Extreme caution must be used during the smoking process, especially around the open clearance light areas, to be certain that insulation and masking paper do not catch fire.

Fig. 8-45. Mike's specialty, a smoked effect, is carefully added with a torch burning acetylene only. Moving fast and close, Mike's pattern is a random but uniform "squiggle." Care is used not to set the truck on fire.

Fig. 8-46. This is what the overall smoked effect looks like. Care must be taken not to scorch the white base coat or effect will be ruined. Entire side took less than 15 seconds to smoke.

Care must also be taken not to scorch the fresh, white paint at this point, as the appearance will be ruined. "Move fast and close with a sorta wiggly motion at the tip trying to keep the smoke effect uniform from one end of the panel to the other," Mike advised. Although the photos don't show how fast Mike moves, it may be helpful to know that laying the smoke pattern on one side of the van took between ten and 15 seconds total—that's moving right along. Study the photographs and then practice on some scrap material until you feel you've mastered the technique well enough to do your vehicle (Fig. 8-46).

SWIRLS

Once the smoking process is complete, Mike added a faint pattern in a swirl effect by first cutting a swirl stencil and then, using a small gun, spraying along the edges of the stencil lightly with the same white acrylic lacquer as the base coat (Fig. 8-47). The effect will vary with the shape and position of

Fig. 8-47. On this particular van, Mike chose to add a faint swirl pattern for even more depth and interest. Stencil is placed next to surface and traced with small gun. White was used to contrast with black smoke.

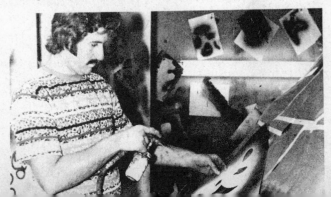

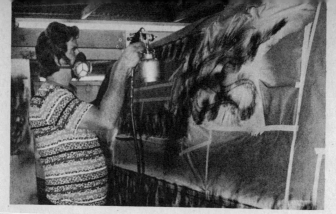

Fig. 8-48. Toners are added next for a rainbow color scheme. Made from well-thinned basic toning colors, they're blended to enhance the van's overall color. Skill and experience are again the key to a successful job here.

the stencil as well as the distance the stencil is held from the van's surface during spraying. Although you may want a repeating pattern, Mike chose to do this van in a random swirl to complement the random smoke effect.

With the smoke and swirl completed, Mike then started to add the colors. Since the van was bronze, Mike chose to make the panels a magenta/red/yellow/orange combination to contrast with the van's exterior color (Fig. 8-48). The toners Mike uses are made from Ditzler Acrylic Lacquer Toning Colors, greatly thinned so that they remain transparent—allowing the smoke and swirl patterns to show through. Again, practice on some scrap before laying on the color, to be sure the toners are sufficiently thinned. Here again, Mike's experience tells him how much and where the toning colors should be sprayed. The end result, however, is a rainbow effect with each color dominant in several areas throughout the panel and with blended areas between providing the transitional mid-tones. Again, practice will help before laying the color on your actual van.

Once the toners have set sufficiently, about a half-hour, the tape lines may be pulled off, exposing the white underbase in those areas previously covered by tape. The outside masking, however, should remain in place until the next step is completed. Using DuPont 756 Clear Acrylic Enamel (acrylic lacquer could be used but Mike feels that the enamel is more durable) mixed with the appropriate hardener according to the directions, the entire panel is coated with one coat, allowed to set briefly, and then followed by a second and heavier gloss coat for the final finish (Fig. 8-49).

148

After sitting overnight, the outside masking paper and tape may be removed and the edges striped if you desire. If you got a little dust in the enamel coat, the finish may be buffed lightly to remove it after curing for two to three weeks *minimum*. Be careful, too, of the striping during the buffing operation, as it comes off very easily.

MURALS

In vanning, as in most other activities, trends come and trends go with astounding and often frustrating regularity—just when you think you're finally 'in,' you're 'out.' One trend that has been around the van scene since the very beginning, though, is still 'in' and from all indications will be 'in' for some time to come. We are referring, of course, to custom-painted van murals.

No two murals are alike—if they were, we'd use decals. But the basic techniques are the same. Let's watch Mike do a sunset-on-a-tropical-lagoon number on this Chevy.

First, the area in which the mural is to be painted is carefully masked off in the desired shape using quarter-inch 3M masking tape. Once the shape is outlined, the remainder of the van—or at least a goodly portion surrounding the mural area—should be masked off with masking paper to prevent overspray from getting to the rest of the paint.

Once masked, the edges of the mural area closest to the tape should be scuffed with 3M General Purpose Pads, stock number 7447, to break the gloss of the original paint and to help stick the masking tape edge more firmly to prevent "bleeds." Once the edges are scuffed, the remainder of the mural area may be sanded with 320 grit wet/dry paper, used dry. This accomplished, the mural area should be blown off with

Fig. 8-49. Once the toners have been applied, the accent tape is pulled, exposing the white beneath. Then acrylic enamel clear is sprayed over everything for protection.

Fig. 8-50. After carefully taping off the area in which the mural is to be placed, sanding well, sealing and application of white "base coat," Mike begins by carefully blending the background colors—sunset oranges in this case—with small spray gun.

high-pressure air to remove sanding dust and then wiped down throroughly with DuPont PrepSol to remove any remaining wax, grease, and fingerprints.

Once the PrepSol has thoroughly evaporated after being wiped off, a coat of Ditzler DL-1970 sealer is shot on according to directions and allowed to dry for about 15 minutes. Mike then uses Ditzler DMA-311 white acrylic lacquer as a base coat for the coming mural. The third light coat should cover well and then be allowed to dry for about a half-hour.

While the white base coat is drying, let's look at some ways you can make your own stencils like those in Mike's elaborate stencil collection—even if you aren't much of an artist. Once you've decided what subjects you want in your mural, wait until your kid brother is looking the other way and rip off some of his coloring books. The designs inside are in simple, bold shapes and are of about the right size for a van mural. Once you find what you want, clip out the page and glue it onto some lightweight cardboard about 15 inches square or larger. When the glue's dry, take an X-Acto knife and carefully trim out the center portion of the picture so that only the outline remains—instant stencil! Don't try to use the page alone, though, as the air pressure from your airbrush will cause the edges to move, creating a ragged and fuzzy outline. No, Mike doesn't use coloring books for stencils, he makes his own—but this'll work.

Fig. 8-51. The horizon line is created by masking off the upper 3/5 (approx.) of the mural area. Mike then blends the colors used in the foreground in the lower 2/5 in accord with the desired effect. In this case blues were used to simulate water.

Once the white base coat is dry, Mike starts the mural by carefully blending colors to create the sky background until a realistic effect is achieved (Fig. 8-50). This takes skill and artistry, and a mistake this early in the game will spoil all the work yet to come. Once the sky area has flash dried, Mike tapes off the horizon line and, in the case of this particular seascape mural, carefully blends colors to simulate the water in the foreground (Fig. 8-51). Both the sky and water are done with well-thinned toning colors that are semi-transparent and allow smooth blending and shading without excessive lacquer buildup.

Fig. 8-52. Mike then starts to create the illusion of "depth" in the mural by adding rocky cliffs to the foreground. Torn cardboard is used as a pattern to be outlined with small gun using black and earthtones. Mike then adds detail and shadow areas freehand with airbrush.

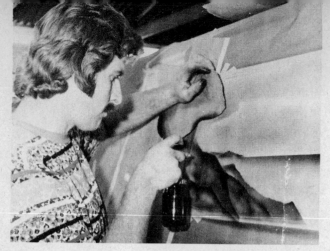

Fig. 8-53. Background mountains are then added in a similar manner—but smaller—in the area above the horizon line. As in the case of the foreground cliffs, the background mountains are then carefully detailed with an airbrush. The illusion of depth is prime goal of these early steps.

Using skillfully shaped stencils, Mike then uses black, browns, blues, etc., to create the mountains that help contain the subject matter of the mural—in this case a sailing ship (Figs. 8-52 through 8-54). To the basic stencil shapes Mike also adds a great deal of freehand detailing with the airbrush, along with much tonal blending and the creation of shadow effects to increase the degree of realism (Figs. 8-55 through 8-58).

Then, using a combination of stencils and free-hand artistry, Mike adds detail after detail, blending and forming the scene until it is complete.

Fig. 8-54. Okay, even though pictured in black and white so that the subtle color blending is not visible, this is what the basic mural area should look like at this point. If you're trying it yourself and aren't happy, try it again. This must be right.

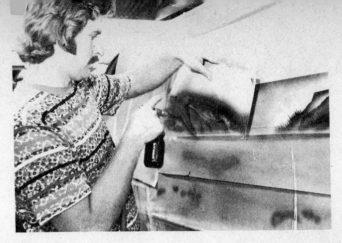

Fig. 8-55. With background done, Mike gets back with the program by starting to add details. Size is critical here to enhance the illusion of depth already established. Things close up should be large while those far away should be small.

The last detail to be added, in most cases, is the sun—or moon—and its rays, to draw the many parts into one unified creation (Figs. 8-59 and 8-60). This done, the completed mural is allowed to dry for about a half-hour, after which the accumulation of overspray is carefully wiped off using a soft cloth—a diaper is great—and the tape covering the white accent lines, if used, is removed (Fig. 8-61). This done, clear acrylic enamel is sprayed over the entire mural area for protection and to bring out the depth of color.

Fig. 8-56. Mike usually adds the "center of interest," in this case a sailing ship, fairly early in the game so that details added later will be in proper perspective. Mike is still using the small gun at this point but beginner may prefer an airbrush—it's safer.

Fig. 8-57. Birds, like the seagulls Mike is adding at this point, can be very helpful in adding a greater illusion of depth. Again size is the key to success in this area. Larger, and thus closer, birds contain more details than those smaller and farther away, too.

After sitting overnight—or whatever length of time is specified by the manufacturer's instructions—the outside masking tape and paper may be removed and the edges striped if desired. To bring out more gloss—especially if clear lacquer was used in place of the clear enamel—the finish may be buffed lightly and carefully after sitting a *minimum* of three weeks. If the edges have been striped, be very careful with the buffer, as the striping will come off very easily.

With each custom paint job Mike includes a set of instructions for the "proper care and feeding" of his custom paint and striping. It says, in essence, that custom paint is as

Fig. 8-58. Still somewhat crude and without much detail, the mural is beginning to take on character and form. Use of the small gun for blending background colors has the added benefit of giving a "mottled" effect—disturbing at first but highly effective.

Fig. 8-59. To help tie the whole scene together, a sun is added next in the appropriate location and light-colored rays painted with the help of a piece of straight cardboard. Rays should be very delicate so as not to over-power the rest of the subject matter.

durable as the original paint as long as it's kept clean, waxed (not polished), and kept away from automatic car washes of all types. High-pressure car washes are especially harmful and must be avoided—a word to the wise.

FLAMES

Flame painting a van—or any vehicle, for that matter—is an operation best left to a professional who has had a great deal of experience with flames. That is, if you want the final detailing of your truck to be up to the rest of the careful work that has gone into it. Nothing short of wiping out the entire

Fig. 8-60. Mike uses one of his "tricks of the trade" here by adding palm trees last to help increase three-dimensional effect. By adding the trees last, it appears as if the rays come through the trees instead of over them. A subtle but highly effective method.

Fig. 8-61. The completed mural still has a slightly "flat" effect due to the accumulation of dry overspray and the rough texture of the lacquer. Once lightly wiped off to remove the overspray and the coated with clear, the feeling of depth is astounding.

right side on a mailbox will ruin the looks of an otherwise bitchin' van worse than a poorly done flame job.

With panel paint and, to some extent at least, with murals, an inexperienced-but-talented painter can usually produce work that rivals that of a full-time professional if enough forethought, care and patience are used during the painting process. With flames, though, the trick lies in the initial layout of the flame design. The design has to be right or everything that follows, regardless of how carefully it's done, is just wasted effort. A little too fat, a little too skinny, a little too stubby, a little too crooked..."a little too" anything will make the finished job "a little too" crummy for your van.

We followed Mike Love around one day while he was applying flames to a customer's new Chevyvan 10. Mike, who has painted hundreds upon hundreds of flamed vans, still takes several hours just laying out the flame design. "It's got to be 'right-on' or my customer just isn't going to be happy," Mike commented. "Even one slip will ruin the whole effect because that one mistake will stand out like a sore thumb. Each flame and each 'lick' has to be perfect or it's all over."

Mike lays out the flame design using quarter-inch 3M masking tape—1/8-inch if the design is small—using care to make sure each side matches the other (Figs. 8-62 and 8-63). Following the initial layout, either Mike or his assistant, Terry, uses one-inch 3M tape to mask the surrounding areas

Fig. 8-62. The initial layout is done with quarter-inch masking tape. This step is critical to overall success.

Fig. 8-63. Sides should be carefully matched for best appearance, especially in the hood and frontal area.

Fig. 8-64. Masking around flames is done with one-inch masking tape. Have plenty, as job takes several rolls.

(Fig. 8-64). Be sure to have plenty of tape available, as this operation usually takes several rolls. Good-quality masking paper is then used to protect the rest of the van from overspray (Fig. 8-65).

Once masked, the flame area is "scuffed" with 3M General Purpose Pads to help paint adhesion as well as to

Fig. 8-65. Top-quality masking paper prevents overspray from sticking to rest of van. Don't skimp here.

insure a crisp tape line (Fig. 8-66). A good dose of DuPont PrepSol applied according to the directions on the can will prevent any wax, grease or fingerprints from ruining the work to come. Be sure you don't touch the area to be painted after wiping off the PrepSol.

A coat of Ditzler DL-1970 sealer should be applied before painting to insure a good bond and to prevent any reaction between the new paint and the old (Fig. 8-67). A couple or three light coats of Ditzler DMA-311 white acrylic lacquer may be applied once the sealer has dried to provide a base coat for the well thinned toning colors that will give the flames their color.

There is no reason on earth, of course, for the flames on your van to be done in the traditional reds and yellows. In fact, the choice of flame colors is very important to the final overall effect, as color will either make or break an otherwise top-quality job. It's probably best to trust the painter here, especially if he's well experienced. One of the best looking flame jobs around was done in lime green on a green car. I doubt very much that the colors were dictated by the owner, but rather suspect that the owner rightly just said, "Do it"—and split.

The van shown in the article was treated to a fairly conventional red/yellow/orange flame job, however, since Mike felt those colors would look best on the maroon van. Starting with well thinned red toning color, Mike used a small gun to carefully paint the recesses and tips of each flame "lick." Experience stemming from hundreds of prior flame

Fig. 8-66. Area to be painted should be carefully scuffed with 3M General Purpose Pads. Gives crisp tape lines.

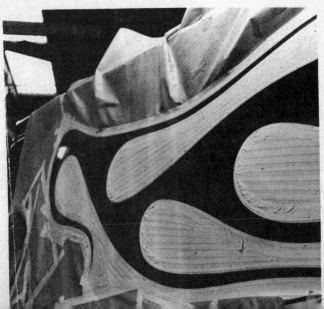

Fig. 8-67. Ditzler DL-1970 sealer is used to help paint adhesion and prevent reaction between new and old paint.

Fig. 8-68. After white base coat has been applied, well-thinned toning colors are put on with small gun.

Fig. 8-69. Final color, yellow, is applied with large gun and helps bring the whole thing together.

jobs pays off here in that the wrong color in the right place will give the flames a "weird" look that gets worse as time goes on. Using the same small gun, only this time filled with orange toning color, Mike blends the area next to the red so that the two colors gradually merge in and out of each other (Fig. 8-68). The final color, yellow, is applied with the big gun and carefully shaded, toned, and blended into the red and orange

Fig. 8-70. A light coating of well-thinned pearl mixed with clear lacquer gives extra brilliance and protection.

Fig. 8-71. Still smiling after thousands of van paint jobs—Mike (right) and Terry of Custom Paint Specialties.

so that every area has some color, but never too much (Fig. 8-69). Mike's skill and experience make it seem easy.

Once the toning colors have been blended to Mike's satisfaction and allowed to "flash" dry, the final touch is added: pearl (Fig. 8-70). For this job Mike chose a red pearl mixed *very sparingly* in clear acrylic lacquer. Several coats were applied to give additional depth to the pearl coating which was, when Mike finished, still only barely discernible. A final "gloss coat" of acrylic lacquer (or acrylic enamel with catalyst if you prefer) winds up the gun work. Once the clear has set, the tape and masking is carefully removed and the van sent out to have the edges striped for the final finishing touch (Fig. 8-71).

Index

Index